Cooking with John Ryan

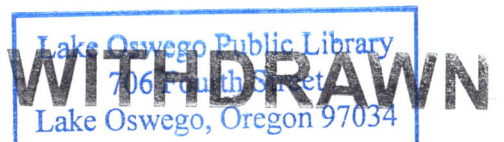

Printed in U.S.A.

ISBN 0-9700069-1-8

Cover and text design by Sheryl Mehary

John Ryan
503 S. W. Colony Drive
Portland, Oregon 97219

Dedication

To Virginia, who asked for this book, my beloved wife, a homemaker, a hostess, and a giver of life and warmth. She sets a table with grace and art, managing the small details, and sets them aright — with no smallness in her heart. A great cook, her taste has been my guide in this haven of happiness we call home.

Table of Contents

Pasta

Pork

Poultry and Game Birds

Seafood

Veal

Vegetables

Acknowledgements and Sources

Candlelight, wine, and laughter all brought me to seeking the mysteries of good food. In Portland in the late 40s and 50s, there were places to go to find what the west afforded: Henry Thiele's, The Benson Hotel (its London Grill is still in the great tradition), Trader Vic's (when they closed it, someone should have rescued the menu of Chinese and Continental dishes), the Old Nendel's, and the special ambiance of Eric Ladd's Kamm House. Italian cooking could be found at Il Travatore, and for hearty homestyle Italian, Mr. Chichini's Monte Carlo and the Lido fed Produce Row, off Grand Avenue, where I worked as a boy.

Jakes' Famous Crawfish was and remains a uniquely preserved link to the early 1900s. When it was acquired by Bill McCormick of Rhode Island, he not only kept its tradition but he created a fish cuisine rivaling any in the U.S.

The clubs that gave me solace were The Multnomah and The University Club.

For atmosphere of old Portland, Jim Louie's Hubers, where his nephew (my friend Andrew Louis) continued the traditions that had the "free lunch" style of pre-Prohibition Portland. Turkey and ham have never tasted better. Andrew's sons still carry on and have preserved this culinary jewel into our times. During Prohibition, I sat with my dad as he and Frank Hanley drank Manhattans from a teapot in cups provided by Jim Louie.

These places taught me about food from my observation. In San Francisco, Jack's, Ermie's, and the North Beach Italians also sparked my culinary curiosity. The Del Prado on Union Square (where the Hyatt now stands) provided Truit Vienne, a delicacy — the menu is lost in the dust of old San Francisco.

My mother was my cooking mentor, not intentionally, but she involved me in the methods of her kitchen. She also prided herself on the appearance of her table, from silver, china and napery.

Art Reiss, chef at the UC (The University Club), took me under his tutelage in the late 50s. His successor, the late Willie Madsen, was always there to answer questions, as was Dan Douda, Maitre d'hôte at the UC's elegant dining room. Craig Vollan, Willy Madsen's successor, is always encouraging and keeps up the UC culinary tradition.

Babs Wilson shares recipes with me. Katie Wendel, my daughter-in-law, and her husband, Dr. Tom Wendel, have taught me the glories of antelope and elk cooked over mountain mahogany at their ranch in Burns. My sister Virginia Golcher is an expert on San Francisco cooking lore. My nephew Tom and his mother, Madeline, have also provided an excellent table. Joe Bianco, award-winning journalist, author, and chef, has been my tutor on Italian cuisine.

Warren Weeks and Jeff Clock at Rio Rico Resort in Arizona have shared food ideas with me. They introduced me to "panko" bread crumbs with flour and egg. See "Orange Roughy" recipe. Panko is a real find. They also introduced me to southwestern delicacies such as "achiote" pork chops.

Most importantly, my wife, Virginia, has helped, guided, and inspired all this and taught me her secrets.

The Books That Helped

Julia Child's *Mastering the Art of French Cooking* has been my cooking bible since 1968. Her most recent, *Julia's*

Kitchen Wisdom, is a compact guide to sauces and cooking times, and a distillation of her cooking and "how to do it" advice.

James Beard's *The James Beard Cookbook* (1959) and his other books instruct on French cooking methods and also old-time American favorites.

George and Bertha Heaters' *Bullcook and Authentic Historical Recipes and Practices* is also good reading and helpful if you are to be cooking game.

Joe Bianco's *Cooking Italian* (Bianco Publishing and Avellino Press) will guide you to the simple steps of Italian cooking, an excellent basis from which to further improvise. His *Treasures Italian* (Bianco Publishing) tells of the cuisines of Bologna, Modena, Mantua, Cremona, Ferrera, and Ravenna, the northeast of Italy below the Veneto and Venice.

Claudia Redon's *The Good Food of Italy, Region by Region* (1990) is a great book for browsing. It discusses Italian food and wine by region and is also an enjoyable travelogue. My friend Judy Buss gave me my copy, which I turn to frequently; her husband, Don, is an adventurous cook and a knowing shopper for vegetables, fruit, fish, and meats.

Wine

The wine writing available will soon fill La Bibliothèque Nationale, but here are two recent guides to French and Italian wines:

French Wines, by Robert Joseph, DK Publishing, Inc., 95 Madison Avenue, New York, NY 10016.

Wines of Italy — The Quality of Life, published by the Italian Institute for Foreign Trade (1994). Request from the Italian Trade Commission, New York City.

Oregon wines are just outside your doorstep; others

can be found by asking at your wine shop. Ask what they have in the $7.00 to $20.00 category. Price is one guide; the vintner or house name, such as "Druohin," "Julius Wile," "Banfi," "Antinori," "Guigal," "Masi," etc., should also be some assurance of quality. Age is relevant in choosing some wines, such as red Bordeaux, Cabernet Sauvignon, Burgundies. With many dry whites, aging past an optimum date will signal deterioration. Ask your wine store for guidance. Don't forget: dry vermouth can be successfully used where a dry white wine is called for in cooking. Remember, vermouth, sherries, ports, Madeiras, Marsalas, etc., are fortified with brandy to 18° and do not spoil.

Try to acquire good table wines at a moderate price. They are there for the asking, but you have to ask. The wines of the Rhône, Chile, Australia, and South Africa await your exploration.

The above shows some of my food and wine prejudices. I hope this helps you to cultivate your own.

Introduction

These recipes have been mainstays of our family cooking for a number of years, and we thought it would be worthwhile to have them available for others to read and perhaps to use in their family cooking. My darling wife, Ginney, suggested I should write them down, so here they are.

Good cooking calls for a recognition of some basic ideas. The first important consideration is heat. Are you using an oven or a gas flame or electricity or cooking on an open hearth with wood or charcoal? Whatever the source of heat, be aware of it and recognize that the distance from the heat and the amount of heat can have a lot to do with cooking success. This means that a certain amount of watchfulness is required while you're cooking. Slow cooking at simmer or moderate heat is the way to tenderness with pot roasts, briskets, rumps, and stews.

With gas heat, it is easy to lower the flame and reduce the heat source if it's causing the food to scorch or burn; or with eggs or cream sauces and other sauces, to curdle or thicken too rapidly. With electricity, remember it is a good device to lift the pan from the heat and reduce the heat before returning the pan to the heat. Otherwise, you will not slow or stop the process.

Sometimes, if overheating is a real problem, go to the sink with your frying pan or saucepan and immerse it in a little cool water for a short while to stop the cooking process or slow it down and control the effect on the food.

This is all pretty much common sense, and an awareness of heat and its effect on cooking is a good beginning, one which is probably not needed by way of advice to experienced cooks.

It is especially important when sautéing garlic and onion in oil for tomato and other sauces that the heat be low to medium, since garlic will burn and taste bitter. The best result with garlic and onions for tomato sauce and other cooking is to cook at very low heat in sufficient oil. The same applies if oil and butter are to be used. Sauté garlic and onions until they are limp or translucent. If garlic browns, simply remove it with a spoon, retaining the flavored oil. Also, when it comes to preparing butter for making, say, a white sauce or a basic flour and butter roux for different sauces, low heat is necessary. Put the butter in to melt; it is sometimes wise to use a small bit of oil with the butter before adding flour. Unsalted butter is great if you can find it at your grocer's. The use of olive oil and less butter reduces the amount of saturated fat in cooking.

As I go along with these recipes, I will discuss my hit-or-miss experiences as a cook for what value they'll have in getting a better result, which is what we're all hunting for.

Sauces, Gravies, Herbs, and Spices

Sauces are often thought of as too difficult for home kitchen cooks. We all can enjoy sauces. They are not complicated, but simple. Start with a basic white sauce or béchamel. The "roux" is flour and butter or butter, oil and flour.

2 tbsp. butter
3 tbsp. flour
1 to 2 cups milk
Salt and pepper
1 pinch nutmeg

Melt butter in saucepan at low heat, then stir in flour, melding the butter and flour. Then pour milk into the roux, whisking or stirring rapidly under moderate heat. Cook to thicken, stirring constantly. Simmer about two minutes. Add salt, pepper and nutmeg.

This is a basic white sauce. Add a cup of chicken broth or bouillon and stir; this is a velouté. For further thickening, add cream or more flour.

Do the same with beef stock, and you have a beef gravy.

Add fish stock from fish poaching, and you have a fish sauce. Fortify with lemon and capers. Check to taste and serve. Clam juice can also serve as a fish stock, though I think it is easy and preferable to make a poaching liquid as appears in recipes for fish in this book.

Any of these sauces can be made, omitting the milk, by adding the appropriate stock to the butter-flour roux. Add heated stock to the roux off the heat, then restore to heat at simmer, stirring to smoothness.

Gravies

Three methods work for me.

1. Add stock to roux as above. If you are using pan juices, deglaze with wine or water — if needed, strain with sieve. Degrease before straining — use bulb or blot with paper to remove grease, or spoon it off.
2. Make a beurre manié, which is flour mixed with butter, then rolled into pellets with your fingers. Add to sauce or gravy to thicken, stir and add more until you reach the right thickness for your sauce. After removing meat from roasting, frying, or sautéing pan, remove pan from heat and splash wine, broth, or water to pan surface, scraping bits from pan with

wooden spoon. The liquid "frizzles" and loosens the meat bits clinging to the pan surface. You then have a basis for your sauce. This process is known as deglazing — in French, "deglaçage."

3. Make a paste of flour and water and add to stock, off the heat. If stock is boiling, it will congeal the flour. Stir so it melds into stock to make a gravy, or mix flour and water in a cup and pour back into the pan to thicken. Also, mix flour and water by shaking in a cup covered with your hand.

A béchamel is the basic roux with milk, as in no. 1 above. Add a grating of nutmeg and pepper and salt to taste. Add chicken stock and you have a velouté. If you want to thicken, add one to two egg yolks off heat and whisk. Do not put yolk mixture over moderate or high heat, or eggs will curdle. This is a rich chicken sauce, also called "Parisian" or "Supreme." I am inclined to skip the egg yolks and use the other methods to thicken the stock.

Mornay or Cheese Sauces

Crumble cheese into white sauce at simmer, stirring as it cooks. It will melt and thicken the white sauce. Taste and season. Gruyère, Parmesan, Mozzarella, Monterey Jack, Cheddar all work well.

Cheddar and 1 tsp. of Worcestershire sauce, plus a cup of beer, 1 tbsp. of Dijon mustard, and 1 tsp. of paprika, make a Welsh rarebit.

Dried Herbs

Parsley, oregano, tarragon, rosemary, basil and Italian herb combinations, French fines herbs, and black pepper-corns are available in quantity. Costco sells them in large containers at far less cost than the small containers available at other stores. Also, grow chives, basil, rosemary, flat leaf and curly parsley in your own herb box garden. Experiment to find the best way to supply your cooking needs without buying the more expensive packages. Flat leaf parsley is preferable for cooking; curly is okay and fine for garnish.

Some "Helpers" or Cook's Secrets You Need to Cook These Recipes

Chicken and beef base (Knorr's and McCormick's are available at most stores in 16-oz. jars). Dilute 1 tbsp. of base in a cup of warm water and heat in microwave 30 to 40 seconds. Use as stock, increasing volume as needed. Most bases are salty, so hold the salt before you use stock. These are a must to add flavor to chicken, beef, and veal sauces. Use these. Canned beef and chicken broths also work well. A can of beef broth added to roast juices makes additional "au jus."

Also use demi glazes to add color and flavor.

In cooking pork, use chicken stock to make your gravy. For turkey, use pan drippings; always degrease.

Equipment

A stainless steel saucepan, nonreactive (doesn't discolor when vinegar, wine, or citrus juices are used). Your fry pan will serve as well, including a nonstick pan. Buy a wooden spoon for stirring butter-flour, etc.

A meat thermometer is helpful. In the recipes that follow are some advised temperatures.

Also, buy a plastic pasta server at your supermarket appliance rack.

Keep or acquire a cast iron skillet and a Dutch oven with cover or similar pan. Casserole dishes of different sizes for lasagnas, stews, scalloped potatoes, etc., will be helpful in your kitchen.

Pyrex and china casseroles are fine, but check with your supplier to get some that can be used on top of the stove as well as in the oven. The ones for the top of the stove can make it easy to thicken juices, etc., after they have been used for cooking in the oven and readying ingredients on top of the stove before putting the casserole in the oven.

Wines in Cooking

I use dry sherry (Christian Brothers and other California wines work well). For the "reds," palatable Merlots, Cabernet Sauvignons, Bordeaux, Côtes du Rhône all serve well. I use "Vendage," a California wine, for cooking, or whatever is left in the uncorked bottle (in our kitchen). The rule is: Use only palatable wine for cooking. If the wine is harsh or tending toward vinegar, it will ruin your sauce or gravy. "Vendage" is a less expensive red or white.

For white cooking wines, use dry sherry for its special taste, or any palatable dry white wine or dry vermouth. Gallo dry vermouth is inexpensive and palatable for cooking. Use where a dry white wine is called for. Save a few drops for your pre-prandial martini, (a congenial custom) use other whites as well.

Salad Dressings

Serves four

1 tbsp. lemon juice
3 tbsp. olive oil
1 tsp. garlic powder
1/4 tsp. sugar (optional)
Salt and pepper

Shake in jar and dressing will emulsify into a creamy appearance. Add to salad just before serving; just coat the lettuce.

Olive Oil and Vinegar (Vinaigrette)

Serves four

2 tbsp. olive oil
1 tbsp. white wine vinegar
1 tsp. dried oregano
1 tsp. dried parsley
1/4 tsp. salt
1/4 tsp. garlic powder
2 grinds pepper from mill
1 tsp. lemon juice (a good squeeze will do)
1 tsp. Dijon mustard, optional, for variety

Shake in jar. Taste. Add dressing to salad just before serving.

La Provence Dressing

1 tsp. garlic, minced
1 cup olive oil
1/2 tsp salt
Ground pepper
1/2 tbsp provence herbs (dried)
1 tsp Dijon mustard
1 egg (whole)
1 tbsp balsamic vinegar
1/2 cup red wine vinegar

Break egg in blender then add all of above but oil. Blend 15 seconds then at high speed. Add oil slowly till well blended.

(Courtesy of La Provence Restaurant, Lake Oswego, Oregon. Efraim Cardenac, John Perrier Belmar, Lisa Soto and "Angie" gave us this recipe.)

Cooking

Be fearless! Use the knives, spoons, etc., suitable for you. Experiment as you cook. Find out what proportions suit your taste. Be attentive! Think about the result as you cook. Check a steak with your fingers. Start with the raw meat. As it cooks, it will be less resistant. Try this for rare, medium rare. Timing is advised. Your own oven, stove, will heat more or less as we advise.

Don't crowd the pan. Taste as you cook. Practice will fortify your culinary judgment.

Have fun, eat well, please your family, guests, and yourself.

Beef

Beef Pot Roast

A Dutch oven, which was also used for vegetable soup in my childhood kitchen, was a staple piece of kitchen equipment. It had a cast iron cover that trapped the heat and cooking moisture but didn't prevent the wonderful aroma of cooking food from filling the kitchen.

For our purposes, any roasting pan with a cover will do, or cover with foil if no cover is available. A cast iron fry pan will do nicely.

Serves 4 to 6

2 1/2 to 3 lbs. chuck beef roast (or other pot roast, ask your butcher)
2 yellow onions, cut into quarters
4 to 5 carrots, cut into 1- to 2-inch chunks
1 cup red wine, white wine or dry sherry (optional)
1 to 2 cups bouillon or beef broth
3 to 4 tbsp. flour
Salt and pepper
3 stalks celery, cut into 1-inch chunks
2 to 3 tbsp. parsley, dried
3 to 4 cloves garlic, coarsely chopped
1 bay leaf
1/2 to 1 small can (8 oz.) of tomato sauce or 1 can (14.5 oz.) diced tomatoes
4 baking potatoes

Take the selected roast and tie it to retain its shape. Dry the roast. Salt and pepper, then flour the roast, rolling it in a plate with the flour.

Heat oil in bottom of pot. Then brown floured roast in pot, turning it to brown on all sides. After browning, remove roast, deglaze pan with wine, and put roast back in pot. Put onion, garlic, bay leaf, sliced carrots, and celery in pot. Then add 2 cups of beef broth, tomato sauce or tomatoes, and wine or sherry.

Bring to boil, then lower the pot to simmer (long cooking tenderizes the meat). Cook covered for 25 minutes a pound at simmer, or in the oven at 325°, covered. The roast should be done in one and three-quarters to two hours, or when fork easily pierces roast.

Check and add additional beef broth as needed as roast cooks.

Additions to Roast (one or all)

Carrots, cut into 1 to 1 1/2 chunks
24 small, peeled onions/2 peeled turnips, halved or quartered (try frozen prepared onions)
String beans
New potatoes

Parboil carrots and turnips (use cooking water to flavor sauce). Then add to meat after one hour; add potatoes and cook about 20 minutes, or boil separately and serve with meat. Thicken gravy with flour-and-water paste.

Variation

Hungarian Pot Roast: Use oregano and 1 tsp. of paprika, and thicken gravy with sour cream.

Serve with potatoes cut into 2-inch chunks and boiled, or with egg noodles.

Beef Stew American Style

Stews, ragouts, etc., are favorites for hunger satisfaction. Besides the Beef Bourguignon recipe given here, we are including a favorite American dish, old fashioned beef stew, together with two lamb stews, a Navarin and Mrs. Riley's Irish stew.

The Navarin has an additional ingredient, turnips, which gives a piquancy to the stew and also introduces us to this wonderful and neglected vegetable. In addition to its use in the Navarin Lamb Stew, try turnips along with roast potatoes or with your next roast, or boil and then puree the turnips and combine them with mashed potatoes, or use them alone in a puree with butter, salt, and pepper.

So, first, we will give the basic Beef Stew American Style.

Serves four

1 1/2 to 2 lbs. beef, cut into 2-inch cubes (chuck, round or other stew meat)
2 tbsp. flour
2 to 3 tbsp. oil, or fat from 3 slices of bacon, cut into 1/4-inch strips and rendered until just crisp
2 cups beef stock or bouillon
1 tsp. thyme, dried
1 tbsp. parsley, dried
1 small can (14.5-oz.) diced tomatoes
Salt and pepper
1 onion, sliced
3 cloves garlic, finely chopped
1 cup red wine (optional)

Preheat oven to 325°.

Use a heavy-bottomed iron skillet or Dutch oven. Put in 2 tbsp. of oil, and by sautéing, render bacon fat, removing crisp bacon, which will be added to stew later. Dry the beef with a paper towel. Salt and pepper, then dredge with flour.

Sauté, sliced onions and chopped garlic in bacon fat, adding oil if needed, until they begin to brown. Remove to a plate, then add floured meat and brown on all sides, stirring with wooden spoon. Sprinkle with thyme and dried parsley, stir for three to five minutes as meat browns on all sides, and add the diced tomatoes, 1 cup of beef bouillon, bacon bits, and reserved onion and garlic. Add the red wine if desired. Cover and place in oven or cook on top of stove. Cook in oven about one hour and test with fork for doneness. If cooking on top of stove, raise to a bubbling boil, then reduce to moderate or low, at simmer, for one hour. In both cases, add the additional bouillon as the stew cooks. When done, thicken if needed with flour-and-water paste (1 tbsp. of flour to 3 tbsp. of water). A tablespoon of butter will smooth the sauce.

Vegetables to Cook with Stew

Cut carrots into 1-inch chunks and add to stew at start of cooking, along with three peeled yellow onions, quartered, and three turnips cut into fourths.

At end of cooking, add one cup of frozen peas; cook for three to five minutes.

String beans, zucchini, etc., can be added at will. Use judgment on when to add the vegetables to cooking stew; some cook faster than others. Celery and celery leaves cut into bite-sized pieces are a must for a good stew. The firmer vegetables will hold their shape during the cooking better than the softer ones, so time when you add the vegetables to the stew. Sliced or wedged cabbage is another suggestion. Sliced or quartered mushrooms and small boiling onions are often added to the basic stew, which would find us back with Beef Burgundy.

Potatoes: I prefer to boil separately and add to dish or stew at end of cooking.

Also good with egg noodles.

Variation: Navarin or Springtime Lamb Stew

Use the basic American Beef Stew recipe above, substituting 2 to 2 1/2 lbs. of lamb stew meat, omitting the red wine. After the stew has cooked for about one-half hour, add six carrots, halved and then cut into 1-inch pieces. Do the same with six peeled turnips and six to 12 peeled boiling onions. See Burgundy Beef Stew, below, for instructions for cooking onions. Add these to stew and cook in oven for another hour. When this is done, strain the stew into a saucepan, remove any bones, and restore meat and vegetables to the sauce.

In the meantime, cook string beans in boiling water, adding frozen peas at the last minute. Beans should be cooked until tender, about ten minutes. Drain beans and peas under cold water to refresh, and add to stew just before serving, basting all vegetables with the sauce and flour and water to thicken, if needed. Garnish with chopped parsley.

Beef Stroganoff

Serves two

9 oz. beef sirloin or tenderloin steak
2 cups beef stock
1/2 tsp. salt
Pepper to taste
2 tbsp. butter
2 tbsp. oil
1 to 2 tsp. Worcestershire sauce
1 onion, medium-sized, minced in processor
1 tbsp. parsley, dried, or 1/2 cup of chopped fresh parsley
1/2 to 1 pt. sour cream
Pasta — Fettuccini or egg noodles for two
1 can mushrooms or 6 fresh, sliced

Slice steak thinly, 1/8-inch thick, then cross-slice to 1-inch bits. Salt and pepper.

Mince onion in processor and sauté in pan with one tbsp. oil. Over low heat, stir, and when limp remove to a plate. Do not brown.

Add butter and remaining oil to pan; raise heat. When butter foams, reduce heat and place sliced beef in pan to sauté briefly to rare — then remove to a plate.

Pour beef stock into pan and scrape bits, then add mushrooms and onion from plate, stir and cook five to six minutes, then add parsley and Worcestershire sauce, and slowly add sour cream, stirring to meld it in sauce for three to five minutes. Restore meat to pan with any juices from plate. Cook further for three to five minutes. Serve over pasta with chopped parsley garnish.

Accompaniments

Boil fettuccini or egg noodles in salted water.
Broccoli is a good accompaniment.

Wine

A Riesling (dry) or Alsatian pinot blanc would be suitable, or a dry Semillon.

Brisket of Beef

My addiction to this delicious dish started at Al Winter's Dunkin's Retreat in Portland on 6th Street, just north of Oak. The back room was for the initiates in off-track betting, poker, etc. Up front there was a cafeteria, as well as the bar and dining room constituting "The Retreat." Al, the son of a judge and a lawyer, gave up the law for bookmaking and being a restaurateur. He had the Pago Pago on Stark Street, a Polynesian nightclub with a clandestine betting parlor above it — The Turf Club — and pioneered in Las Vegas when he built The Sahara just shortly after Bugsy erected The Flamingo.

This dish used to be a favorite in kosher restaurants as well.

Serves four

1-1/2 lbs. beef brisket
2 onions, peeled
4 to 6 whole cloves stuck in peeled onions
1 stalk celery with leaves, cut into 1 inch chunks
8 carrots, peeled, cut into 1-1/2 inch chunks
4 cloves garlic, unpeeled
2 to 3 tbsp. flour for thickening
6 peppercorns
1 bay leaf
2 tsp. salt
2 sprigs parsley (on string — immerse in broth)
10 cups water (enough to cover brisket and vegetables)

Use a deep pot. Heat water in pot. Bring to boil. Score any fat on brisket and immerse in pot. Remove the grey scum that rises on first cooking (use a large spoon for this).

Then add vegetables and spices, but add carrots after one and one-half hours of cooking. Add onion, garlic, cloves, celery, peppercorns, and salt. Lower to simmer and cook two to three hours. Check for tenderness with tines of fork.

When done, remove brisket to warm oven on a plate with a little broth to moisten.

Test broth and add beef base if needed. Remove carrots, onions, and celery with slotted spoon. Pour broth for gravy through strainer or slotted spoon into saucepan. Discard bay leaf, cloves, garlic and peppercorns. Thicken with 2 tbsp. of flour mixed with 3 tbsp. of water. Cook to thicken. Add salt and pepper to taste.

Cut brisket cross-gain in slices. Serve with mashed or boiled potatoes, carrots, and onions.

Spoon gravy over sliced brisket.

Burgundy Beef Stew

Beef Stew with Red Wine, Onions, Bacon and Mushrooms

My first and only trip to Burgundy was in 1954, traveling northward to Lyon. A lasting memory is of the hills in late September turning to their autumn colors with the clouds shifting and granting the earth momentary showers. Now that Oregon has become famed for its pinot noirs, the red wine grape of Burgundy, I realize the great similarity of the hills and weather of Burgundy with those in Oregon's Multnomah, Marion, Yamhill, and Washington counties. In 1954 in Oregon, wine and the vintner's art were confined to a few fruit wines, and wine bibbers were very few. These were mostly expatriates from California or those who made wine for their own table use. In Oregon we have made great progress in wine making and in gastronomy. But the American cooking of my heritage and yours is of the best.

Many of the recipes and methods in this collection are part of my tutelage learned by a watchful boy in my mother's kitchen.

Serves four

6 slices of bacon, blanched, simmered in 1 qt. of boiling water; or, if available, a 6-oz. slab of bacon, sliced, together with its detached rind; blanch the same way

2 lbs. stewing beef (top round, chuck or sirloin), cut into 2-inch chunks

1 carrot, sliced

1 onion, sliced

3 cups dry red wine (pinot noir or other red — pinot noir is the grape of red Burgundy)
2 to 3 cups brown beef stock or canned beef bouillon
1 tsp. salt
1/2 tsp. pepper
2 tbsp. flour
1 tbsp. tomato paste, or 1/2 can (8-oz.) of tomato sauce
2 to 3 cloves garlic, finely chopped
1/2 tsp. dried thyme
1 bay leaf, crumpled
The blanched bacon rind (optional)
12 to 14 peeled white small onions
8 to 12 mushrooms, sliced and sautéed in 1 tbsp. of butter
2 to 3 tbsp. olive or other oil

Dutch oven or fireproof casserole, usable on top of the stove, 3 to 4 inches deep

Preheat oven to 450°

Preparing the Onions

With a small knife, cut a cross in the stem of each onion and then drop all onions into boiling water for three to four minutes and lift out with spoon. When cool enough to handle, pare off outer leaves.

Fifteen minutes before stew is done, cook in boiling water with 1 tsp. of oil and 1 tsp. of salt, then drain and sauté in 1 tbsp. of butter and salt and pepper to taste. Onions will be added when beef is ready.

Preparing the Bacon

Cut bacon into lardons or slices 1 inch by 1/4 inch. Leave rind whole.

Boil water in pan and place bacon and rinds in pan, or bacon only if you don't have rind. Blanch* the bacon for three to four minutes, remove, and dry on paper towels. Then place in casserole or Dutch oven with 1 tbsp. of olive or other oil and sauté the bacon and rind for about three minutes to brown it lightly. Remove to side dish.

*To blanch: Cook in water to get rid of preservative. Also, use cold water to refresh beans, peas, etc., and to slow down cooking.

Browning the Meat

Salt and pepper the meat and have oil in pan just smoking. Put the meat in the pan and sauté it until all sides are brown. Then remove the meat to the side dish with the bacon.

The Vegetables and the Meat

Next, brown the sliced vegetables in the oil in the pan and then return the meat and bacon to the pan, adding salt and pepper and 2 tbsp. of flour, tossing the meat with the flour. Then take pan from top of the stove and place it in oven to brown for three to five minutes. After the flour browns, reduce the heat to 325°. Remove pan and add herbs, garlic, tomato paste, wine, and beef stock. Place in oven to cook for 2 to 3 hours, testing with fork for tenderness. When fork pierces easily, meat is done. Remove pan to top of stove and pour contents into a sieve. Remove rind and all but meat from sieve and put meat back in pan with juice.

Mushrooms and Finishing the Dish

Slice mushrooms and sauté in butter and oil. Then place these in pan with onions, basting them in the sauce. Place back in oven for a few minutes to let the sauce marry the mushrooms and onions, and then we are ready to eat. Serve with boiled potatoes, noodles, or rice. Garnish with chopped parsley.

This is quite an effort, but it is its own reward. Good eating!

Wine

A French Burgundy, a Chianti or a Côtes du Rhône, or an Oregon pinot noir are all good company for this hearty meal. (An Erath or a Ponzi pinot noir from Oregon are old reliables.)

Corned Beef and Cabbage

Serves four to six

This is celebrated as an Irish dish and was a staple of Maggie and Jiggs in the cartoon of my childhood, all but forgotten now. It is also a favorite of Mary Bosch.

In 1945 I saw this cooked over a turf (peat) fire in a pot over the open hearth at my cousin Dave Ryan's farm in Doon, County Tipperary.

Use the same directions as used in brisket of beef. Corned beef is just a brisket cured in brine, etc. Cooking time is two and one-half to three hours.

Cut cabbage into wedges. Also add cooking spices in packaged corned beef and 2 bay leaves, or if no package of spices use 1/2 tbsp. of allspice, five peppercorns, 2 tbsp. dried parsley, and two bay leaves.

Add the cabbage and carrots 2 hours into the cooking.

Remove the beef and vegetables after two and one-half to three hours.

Serve with boiled, buttered potatoes; cabbage; and a mustard sauce.

Here is my recipe for the mustard sauce:

6 tbsp. Dijon mustard
1 tsp. prepared horseradish
2 to 3 tsp. cream or half-and-half
1/2 tbsp. dried parsley for garnish
2 tbsp. butter

Melt butter in saucepan over low heat, then stir in mustard and horseradish, add cream, and blend. Taste and modify to taste by adding more cream if too zesty for your taste. Sauce should be thick enough to drip from a spoon.

Serve on plate with sliced corned beef, cabbage wedges, carrots, and buttered potatoes. Pour sauce on slices of beef.

Beer is the best to wash it down. It is a sturdy and satisfying dish. Erin go bragh!

Filet Mignon with Red Wine Sauce

Bifteck Sauté Marchand du Vins

This is the wine merchant's sauce flavored simply with the deglazed steak flavor, shallots or green onions (minced) and a swirl of butter. The sautéed mushrooms can then be blended in or served on the side. In this version, I serve them on the side, but blending is also good and looks pretty when spread on the steak, commingling the flavors of wine, onions, mushrooms, butter, and beef glaze.

Serves two

2 Filet Mignon, 1 1/2 inches thick
4 tbsp. cooking oil, divided
Salt and pepper
Garlic powder
6 mushrooms, sliced
2 tbsp. dried parsley or 1/2 cup chopped, fresh parsley
4 tbsp. shallots or green onions, minced, divided
4 to 6 red new potatoes
2 to 3 tbsp. butter
1 bunch spinach, washed
2 oz. red wine
1/4 cup bouillon or beef stock and water (if needed)

Dry filets with paper towel. (A dry meat surface is needed for browning.) Salt and pepper and sprinkle with garlic powder. Press in with heel of your hand. Put fry pan or sauté pan on moderate heat with 2 tbsp. of cooking oil. Cook one side about six minutes and turn, cooking the other side two to three minutes, to medium rare. Press thumb into steak to test for doneness. When there is still "give," it is either rare or medium rare. When filets are done as desired, remove to warm plate and keep warm.

Meanwhile: Put 2 tbsp. of oil in pan with 2 tbsp. of minced shallots or green onions. Cook at low heat for two to three minutes, add sliced mushrooms and a pat of butter, and cook until tender.

Slice peeled red potatoes in half and place in boiling salted water. Test with sharp knife for doneness (about 15 minutes cooking time). Drain and put in 2 tbsp. of butter and parsley, chopped or dried, and shake in pan.

Just before all other items are cooked, put spinach in pan with 2 inches of boiling water and cook for one to two minutes. Then drain and press with slotted spoon. When liquid seems removed, salt and pepper and add a splash of olive oil, a grating of nutmeg, and a squeeze of lemon. It is ready to serve. Stir lightly with fork to mix oil, lemon, nutmeg, and spinach.

Next: When filets have been removed from pan, deglaze with red wine, then add 1 tbsp. of butter and 2 tbsp. of minced shallots or green onions to pan.

Stir with wooden spoon for one to two minutes, then cook briefly. Add butter to thicken sauce, as needed.

Place potatoes, spinach, and one filet on each plate. Either serve mushrooms on side or mingle them with the wine sauce. If you add bone marrow to the wine sauce, as is, it will be a bordelaise sauce.

Wine

This was cooked at Riverpoint in 1996. Virginia selected a Mouton Cadet, Bordeaux red to go with this dinner. (An Erath Vineyards, Dundee, Oregon, pinot noir is a good alternative.)

Bon chance and bon appetit.

Prime Rib of Beef

This cut of beef is an elegant dish. If oven heat and timing are correctly observed, it will provide your family with a delicious dinner, and for a party, one that will please your guests, sending them a message of welcome.

Serves four.

3 to 4 lbs. standing prime rib
Salt and pepper
1 onion, peeled and quartered, optional
Garlic powder

Preheat the oven to 325°.

Temperatures per thermometer: 120°F for rare, 130°F for medium rare; or at oven temperature of 325°F for 13 to 15 minutes a pound.

Ribs 8–12 are favored cut. Ribs 1–4 (from shoulder to loin) have fat and cap of meat before you get down to the ribeye, all edible but not as fine as ribs 8–12. If your roast is smaller than five ribs, preheat oven to 450° and cook meat to brown at 450° for 15 minutes, then reduce to 325°.

Dry the rib roast and salt and pepper to taste; sprinkle with garlic powder. Place roast in roasting pan, fat side up. Cook meat for 13 to 15 minutes a pound for medium rare; add the quartered onion pieces to the pan (they add to the flavor of the juice).

When cooking time in oven is up, remove roast to platter or slicing board for 10 to 15 minutes. Place roast onions beside roast. Lower heat in oven so it is available for warming roast if needed. The juice from the pan should be strained into a warm sauce boat. Supplement with beef broth and red wine if needed.

Accompaniments

Au jus from pan: Pour over sliced beef.

Mashed potatoes: Boil four peeled baking potatoes, sliced 1/8-inch thick, in salted water for 15 to 20 minutes; drain, mash, and add two to three pats of butter, salt, pepper, and 1/4 cup of warm milk. Mash and fluff.

Green peas (frozen) in pan with water and thin slices of onion: Quickly boil three to five minutes. Refresh under cold water, drain, and return to stove at warm, adding a pat of butter, salt, and pepper. Shake in pan, then keep warm for serving.

String beans, peas and carrots, pureed potatoes and turnips are other suggestions.

Place beef slices, one quarter of a roast onion, mashed potatoes, and buttered peas on a plate; spoon jus on beef, or, instead of potatoes serve with white rice.

Carving: Avoid thick slices; thin slices are more flavorful.

Rump Roast

This was a favorite of Virge Ryan's kitchen. We would buy the meat from Raucher's Butcher Shop on NE 7th Street, and we would roast it at 325° in a preheated oven for 22 to 25 minutes a pound. Twenty-two minutes should turn out medium rare. Roast potatoes; carrots (cut into chunks); and quartered, peeled onions in pan.

Serves four

3 lbs. rump roast
3 tbsp. oil
3 tbsp. flour
1 to 2 tbsp. butter
4 onions, quartered
8 carrots, cut into chunks
3 to 4 baking potatoes, peeled and sliced into 1-inch slices, or small reds
3 slices bacon, blanched in boiling water for 3 minutes (optional)
Salt and pepper
2 cloves garlic, chopped
1-2 cups beef broth
1/2 cup red wine (optional)

Preheat oven to 325°.

Dry roast and salt and pepper it. Place small slivers of garlic in any folds of roast. Flour a plate and roll roast in it, including ends.

Blanch bacon in boiling water for two to three minutes. Reserve one slice of the blanched bacon.

Dry blanched bacon and sauté in roasting pan on top of stove, rendering some of its fat. Add 2 tbsp. of olive oil.

Brown and sear roast in this, then remove from heat. Add 1 cup of beef broth and place roast in oven. Cook for a little over two hours — cover roast for the first one and one-half hours, and cook uncovered for remainder. Place reserved strip of blanched bacon on top of roast. When cooking reaches one and one-quarter hours, put carrots and onions in with roast.

Oven-brown potatoes in separate pan (40 minutes cooking time). Place in Pyrex with 1 tsp. of oil. Roll potatoes in oil, salt, and pepper. Shake or turn potatoes several times while they are cooking.

Remove roast to platter; let roast stand. Turn down oven to warm. Put vegetables on a dish and keep warm in oven.

Gravy

Heat pan, add beef broth if needed, plus 1/2 cup of wine, if desired. Stir pan to loosen bits on bottom of pan. Thicken with 1 to 2 tbsp. flour in equal amount of warm water, or make beurre manié pellets, working butter and flour together, then adding them to gravy. Butter makes for a smoother, more silken sauce.

Accompaniments

Slice one head of cabbage; put in pan with 1/2 water and 1/2 milk just to cover. Add 1 1/2 tsp. of salt and two grinds of black pepper. Heat to boil, then simmer 15 minutes. Drain with slotted spoon to serve. (Try the milk and water cabbage bouillon — it tastes great!)

Wine

Any good table red will suit this dish, or beer will also be a pleasant drink.

Steak Diane

Serves two

6 tournedos of beef, cut 1/4-inch, flattened between pieces of wax paper (filet preferred)
Salt and pepper
1/4 stick butter
2 tbsp. olive oil
3/4 cup beef stock or bouillon
2 tsp. cornstarch
2 tsp. Dijon mustard
1/2 lemon
Worcestershire sauce to taste
2 to 3 mushrooms, sliced
2 tbsp. dry sherry
2 to 3 scallions, finely chopped
1/4 cup fresh parsley, finely chopped, or 1 tbsp. of dried parsley
1 oz. cognac or other brandy

Cut tournedos and flatten between pieces of wax paper. Finely chop scallions and parsley and place on a plate to the side. Put olive oil and butter in sauté pan or fry pan at moderate heat. Salt and pepper tournedos. When butter foams, lay the meat in the pan; cook 1-1/2 to 2 minutes each side, turning to cook. Pour cognac over meat and light it — use a butane lighter or a long match and keep back from the pan as it flames. Shake pan. When flame subsides, remove meat to warm plate.

Sauce Diane

Have mixed 1/2 cup of beef stock with 1 tsp. of Dijon and cornstarch or flour. Put scallions and parsley in pan and stir for two to three minutes. Add the beef stock-mustard-starch mix and stir as it cooks.

Squeeze the juice of half of a lemon; add a liberal sprinkle of Worcestershire sauce plus mushrooms. Cook for two to three more minutes. Add dry sherry. Reduce sauce to desired thickness.

Return meat to sauce, basting it. Then serve.

Swiss Steak

This was prepared for Virginia at Gearhart in August 1996, and since then we have enjoyed it in its many variations. My mother, Virge Ryan, was an expert at this dish, a transformation of an inexpensive cut of beef to a delicacy, blending vegetables, meat and all into slow-cooked savor.

Serves four

1 1/2 lbs. top round or other roundsteak — have butcher tenderize, or put steak between two pieces of wax paper and tenderize with mallet
4 carrots, chopped into 1-inch chunks, splitting thick chunks lengthwise
3 tbsp. dried parsley or 1/2 cup fresh, chopped
1 yellow onion, thinly sliced
3 to 4 cloves garlic, peeled and finely chopped
1 tsp. dried thyme (optional)
1 cup red wine (optional)
Olive oil as needed (about 3 tbsp.)
1 to 2 cups beef bouillon or beef broth from beef base
1 can (8-oz.) tomato sauce, or 1 can (14.5-oz.) diced tomatoes
Salt and pepper
Garlic powder
3 stalks celery, finely chopped or processed
Flour as needed

Preheat oven to 325°.

Cut the tenderized steak into serving-size pieces. Sprinkle with garlic powder. Salt and pepper, then dredge with flour on both sides of meat. Reserve. In a cast iron skillet or other roasting pan, put 3 tbsp. of oil (my choice is olive oil), turn up the heat until the oil just sizzles, and place the cut meat in the pan. Then reduce the heat. Watch the heat so as not to burn the surface. Brown on both sides. When brown, remove to a plate or pan to warm in the oven. Add oil and sauté the sliced onion and chopped garlic at low heat, stirring until they become translucent. Do not brown — but it's okay if you do. Return the meat to the pan. Pour 1 cup of beef bouillon or broth into the pan, add a cup of red wine together with a tablespoon of flour, and stir into the mix.

Place carrots and celery with a slice or two of onion in another pan with water to cover. Parboil the vegetables for about 10 minutes, then add to the roasting pan with the meat, using the water from the vegetables to add to the cooking sauce, together with the processed celery. Put in the oven and cook for an hour or better, testing the meat with a fork for tenderness. Add broth to thin if sauce gets too thick. Water is also okay as you sip for flavor.

This can also be done in a covered pan on top of the stove, cooking at a simmer for 1-1/2 to 2 hours. Be sure you add liquid if you simmer on the stovetop. This avoids scorching.

Serve with rice or boiled potatoes.

Wine

Our cellar had some good reds to keep company with this rich sauce. These were offered Virginia: La Vieille Ferme, Rhône Valley 1996, Ca' del Solo, Big House Red 1998, California Red, Cabernet Sauvignon, Vin de Pays D'Oc, George Duboeuf 1998, Chateau Salitis, Carbades 1996. Virginia selected La Vieille Ferme. We want no sympathy in our adversity.

Whole Roast Tenderloin or Sirloin Boquetierre

This is a festive party dish and can be prepared before the guests arrive. The "Boquetierre" refers to vegetables that add color to the serving, a "bouquet."

A sirloin roast is a little less expensive, and just as succulent.

Have the butcher tie the roast for even size in cooking.

Serves six

3 to 4 lbs. whole tenderloin or sirloin roast, tied by butcher
3 tbsp. melted butter
1 tbsp. oil (with butter)
Salt and pepper
1 tsp. garlic powder

Vegetables — for six people

1/2 lb. string beans
1/2 lb. small carrots
18 new potatoes, peeled
3 tomatoes, sliced in half
1 tbsp. bread crumbs (for tomatoes)
1 tbsp. chopped parsley (for tomatoes)
1 tbsp. dried oregano (for tomatoes)
3 tsp. olive oil
1 tsp. garlic powder
1 tbsp. powdered Parmesan cheese
Salt and pepper

Preheat oven to 400°.

Vegetables

Prepare vegetables to garnish the roast: Cut tomatoes in half and sprinkle salt, pepper, garlic powder, oregano, and parsley on each tomato. Sprinkle all with olive oil. Top off with powdered Parmesan. Place in oven in separate pan as roast cooks; cook 15 minutes and remove.

Mushrooms

12 mushrooms, sliced, for sauce

Prepare in pan with oil and squeeze of lemon. Add to sauce at end of preparation.

Roast

Place tenderloin 6 inches under broiler. (For roast sirloin, cook as for prime rib of beef. See recipe on page 32.)

Insert meat thermometer. Baste with melted butter and oil. Remove when thermometer reads 120°F.

Deglaze pan with red wine, Madeira, or dry sherry. Add beef stock to sauce; thicken with butter and flour. Add mushrooms.

Arrange platter with vegetables surrounding sliced tenderloin in 1/8-inch slices, the same for sirloin. Pour sauce over slices on each plate. Garnish with a sprinkle of dried parsley.

Wine

A Ponzi, Oregon pinot noir, the Cabernet Sauvignons, or the richer dry reds will suit this dish.

Lamb

Braised Lamb Shoulder

Serves two

4 lamb shoulder chops, 1 1/4 inches
1 green pepper, washed and sliced in half. Remove seeds and ribs, then slice into 2-inch pieces
3 to 4 garlic cloves, chopped
1/2 onion, sliced thinly
5 to 6 mushrooms, sliced
Olive oil in pan as needed
Garlic powder
Salt and ground pepper to taste
2 chopped fresh tomatos or small can (14.5 oz.) of diced tomatoes
1 tbsp. dried oregano
1 tbsp. dried parsley
3 oz. dry sherry

Preheat oven to 350°.

Dry chops and sprinkle with garlic powder, parsley and oregano, pressing the herbs into the flesh of the chops. Heat 2 to 3 tbsp. of olive oil in a cast iron skillet until oil begins to smoke. Put chops in skillet and lower heat to medium to brown chops on both sides. When chops are just golden, pour cup or better of dry sherry into pan and over chops. Put pepper slices on top of chops, together with onion slices and chopped garlic and tomatoes. Cover skillet and place in oven. Foil will do for a cover. Cook for 45 to 50 minutes. Test meat with a fork for tenderness as it cooks. Spoon juices to baste meat and add a little sherry to keep sauce liquid.

Accompaniments

Serve with rice or boiled potatoes with broccoli or spinach, olive oil and a squeeze of lemon. If carrots are desired, peel and slice them into 1-inch pieces and cook with meat after preboiling them for ten minutes.

Wine

A Vieille Ferme Côtes du Rhône or Robert Mondavi Coastal Cabernet Sauvignon will complement this Provençal-inspired dish. Try this for a romantic evening.

Lamb Chops with Sherry Sauce

Serves two

4 lamb chops
1/4 tsp. garlic powder
Salt
Freshly ground pepper
1/4 tsp. oregano, per chop
1 tbsp. parsley, dried
1 to 2 tbsp. olive oil
2 oz. dry sherry
1 to 2 tsp. Worcestershire sauce
1 tbsp. butter

Prepare chops. Dry, salt and pepper, then press garlic powder, dried oregano, and parsley on each chop.

Put of olive oil in a pan and heat to sizzle. Place chops seasoned side down, and reduce heat. After three minutes, check to determine if they are browned properly, then turn and cook four to five minutes. Press chop with finger. If it gives with slight resistance, it should be rare or medium rare. Cut into a chop to be sure it is done to your satisfaction.

Remove chops to plate. Deglaze the pan with dry sherry, scraping bits from pan, then add butter and Worcestershire sauce and pour over chops on serving plate.

Accompaniments

Serve with mashed potatoes or scalloped potatoes. Peas, green beans, or little carrots, glazed, are suggested.

Wine

A Bordeaux, Cabernet Sauvignon, merlot, or Italian reds, all complement the lamb.

Mrs. Riley's Lamb Stew

Mrs. Riley was a fine, silver-haired woman, the mother-in-law of my aunt, Eva Mulcahy Riley. Eva's husband was Frank Valentine Riley, the gasman. Frank was a source of information on neighborhood happenings, information that he garnered as he fixed gas appliances in the northeast and north of Portland. He was also a very loyal friend. Mrs. Riley invited Mother, Daddy, and me (aged six at most) to an early lunch before we started off to the North across the Columbia River on the old one-span Interstate Bridge of the pre-freeway world of the late 1920s.

I can't remember the destination of our journey, or anything else but the taste of her wonderful stew, lovingly prepared for her friends. I also remember my mother and father's gratitude. Below is my reconstruction of the ingredients and the cooking. (Mr. Riley, the host, told me about seeing the Sioux warriors on horseback in the 1890s in the Dakota Territory.)

Serves four

2 lbs. lamb stew meat (short ribs, shoulder, breast, neck; ask your butcher for mix for stew — cook bones and all)
4 cups water, or 2 cups each of water and chicken broth
3 carrots, diced
3 stalks celery, diced
1 cup onion, chopped, diced
Salt and pepper
12 small boiling onions, peeled
2 cups frozen peas
12 small red potatoes, peeled and cut in half
1 cup cream (optional)

4 tbsp. butter
4 tbsp. flour
2 tbsp. chopped parsley or dried parsley for garnish;
save 3 to 4 parsley stalks for bouquet garni
1/4 tsp. thyme
3 to 4 peppercorns
Celery leaves
Cheesecloth for bouquet

Prepare carrots, onion, and celery. Sauté briefly in a soup pan with 1 tbsp. of butter. When wilted or limp, pour water, or water and chicken broth, in pan over carrot-onion-celery mix and bring to boil.

Meanwhile, wash lamb and cut into bite-sized pieces (about 1 inch by 1 inch). Salt and pepper, then place meat with bones in boiling water. Continue boiling and skim until grey matter no longer rises, then reduce to simmer. Cook for 1-1/2 hours.

Make bouquet garni of three parsley stalks, one bay leaf, four peppercorns, 1/2 tsp. of dried thyme, and some celery leaves. Place these in a washed cheesecloth bag, tie bag with string, and immerse in the broth with the string outside the pan for later withdrawal. (Parsley stalks only to prevent discoloring of final sauce.)

Boil potatoes seperately. Add them to broth after broth is strained, when cooking is completed.

Immerse onions in boiling water in another pan for three to five minutes. Remove with slotted spoon and, when cool enough to handle, peel. Leaves should come off easily. Cut a cross in stem ends. Place onions in sauté pan in 1-1/2 cups of water and bring to boil, then down to simmer. Test with fork after 15 minutes. Drain and set aside. Save water to add to broth, if needed.

After broth cooks for about 1-1/2 hours, test meat with fork and, if it yields easily, remove from heat.

Prepare a roux of 2 tbsp. flour in 2 tbsp. of butter at low heat in saucepan. Stir until roux is melded, then strain the broth into roux, stirring with wooden spoon. Remove meat from sieve and place on plate to warm. Press down on vegetables to get juice into pan, and then discard bones and bouquet garni. Return meat to mixture. (It is an option to add 1 cup of cream to stew and additional flour if needed for thickening.)

Meanwhile, sauté onions in 1 tbsp. of butter, salt, and pepper. When heated through, pour onions into stew. While stew is bubbling, add 2 cups of frozen peas and cook further for three minutes. Ladle onto plate with sufficient potatoes for each serving. Serve with French bread or biscuits.

Accompaniments

If you desire an additional vegetable, cook four carrots, sliced, in 1 1/2 inches of water with salt, pepper, and 1 tsp. of sugar. When cooked al dente (chewy to the bite), drain and swirl in 1 tbsp. of butter, garnishing with a sprinkle of dried parsley. Serve on side of plate.

Erin go bragh and God bless Mrs. Riley!

Rack of Lamb

Serves four

2 racks of lamb, cut into four pieces — 3 to 4 ribs per person
1 tbsp. oregano, dried
1 tbsp. parsley, dried
1/2 tbsp. garlic powder
1 tbsp. olive oil
Salt
Ground pepper
1 tbsp. butter

Preheat oven to "broil."

Divide the racks into four serving sizes, two to three chops per person.

Dry, then salt and pepper (freshly ground), pressing pepper, oregano, and parsley into racks. Sprinkle with garlic powder and then roll in olive oil. Place in shallow roasting pan. Place rack bone side up and broil for ten minutes. Turn and broil for 20 to 30 minutes more until fat side is browned and rack is rare or medium rare (120° to 130° for rare; 140° for medium rare).

Remove rack to platter or cutting board. Slice portions, separating each chop.

Add juices to pan and deglaze with dry sherry (2 oz.) or Madeira or red wine. Add chicken stock to extend the sauce with 1 tbsp. of Worcestershire and butter to thicken.

Serve chops with potatoes and a vegetable.

Roast Leg of Lamb

Serves four to six

3 to 4 lbs. of leg of lamb, trimmed of fat and bones
1 clove garlic, cut into slivers
3 tbsp. vegetable or olive oil
2 tbsp. salt
1 tsp. freshly ground pepper
2 onions, thinly sliced
2 carrots, thinly sliced
1-1/2 cups beef or chicken stock
1 tbsp. lemon juice
Optional: sprinkle dried oregano on lamb for a mediterranean touch

Preheat the oven to 350°.

Tie boned leg of lamb, placing slivers of garlic in fold and also in fat. Use knife to insert.

Salt and pepper roast. Brush the lamb with oil and lemon juice, mixed. Insert a meat thermometer in thickest part of the leg.

Place leg fat side up on a rack in roasting pan and roast, uncovered, for 20 minutes, then scatter onions and carrots in pan and roast for another 40 to 60 minutes, or when thermometer reads 140° for medium rare, 125° to 130° for rare, or 120° for blood rare. For four pound roast 14 to 18 minutes per pound should produce rare roast.

Remove roast to platter. Deglaze the pan with red wine, sherry or Madeira. Add chicken or beef stock to pan, heat, and scrape pan. Add lemon juice, heat, then strain into sauce boats, pressing down on vegetables to extract juices, and discard. Skim fat and serve.

Accompaniments

Serve with mashed or roast potatoes and glazed carrots and peas. String beans are also good.

Wine

A good Rhône wine, Chianti, Cabernet Sauvignon, or red Bordeaux will go well with the lamb.

Pasta

Note Sauce Bolognese can be found in the section on vegetables, (See page 159).

Capellini with White Sauce and Ham, Mushrooms, Peas and Cheese

Serves two

2 tbsp. flour
3 tbsp. butter, divided
3 slices mozzarella cheese
2 tbsp. Parmesan, grated
1 cup heated milk
1 can (12-oz.) mushroom slices
2 tbsp. oil, divided
2 slices precooked ham, sliced into small pieces, 1 inch by 1/2 inch
1 cup chicken broth
1 jar pimientos
1-1/2 cups frozen peas
3 oz. dry sherry
2 tbsp. dried parsley
2 to 3 gratings nutmeg
1 shallot, minced or finely chopped
2 portions capellini pasta (more if more than two servings desired)

Make béchamel: flour, 2 tbsp. of butter, melted and stirred in saucepan, then slowly add warmed milk, stirring or whisking away lumps. Add nutmeg, salt, and pepper. Add, in bits and pieces, Mozzarella and grated Parmesan; stir to liquefy, then add 1 oz. of sherry and continue to simmer.

Place 1 tbsp. of oil and 1 tbsp. of butter in another sauté pan over medium heat. When it liquifies, add minced shallots and cook for three to four minutes, then add mushrooms, stir and coat at low heat with dry sherry, reduce, and set aside to add to pasta later.

In frying pan with 1 tbsp. of olive oil, sauté ham pieces at low heat, stirring with wooden spoon. Do not cook to a crisp, but heat through and then set aside on a plate to be added to the pasta later.

Cook pasta, then drain, saving 2 cups of the cooking water. In large sauté pan, mix ham with pasta, add pimientos and frozen peas; continue to stir. Add shallots and mushrooms.

Heat béchamel sauce after tasting for flavor. Add 1 cup of the cooking water or better to keep pasta from sticking. Add sherry to bèchemel if needed, then mix in the pasta, ham, peas, pimentos and mushrooms. If it is needed, add some more of the cooking water. Serve on plates and sprinkle with dried parsley.

Wine

Try pinot gris from Flynn Vineyards, Dallas, Oregon, or a Côtes du Rhône (Guigal) to complete this feast. Just a selection; what's in your own cupboard should do very nicely.

Lasagna

Lasagna is the name of a pasta, wide, slightly corrugated on the sides. It also is a general term embracing various dishes of layered pasta covered with ground meat and cheese baked in a casserole.

Here is a recipe for one of many of these delicious and filling dishes. We made this to please our guests the Heaths. It takes some time, and I started in the afternoon for preparation. It burbled unheard in a very low oven while we entertained them on the porch of the Rio Rico Resort overlooking San Cayatano Mountain and the Santa Cruz Valley. As we watched a clear blue evening sky, an enormous white moon rose from behind the mountain, casting a spell over us. Laughter and tinkling ice made us forgetful of the oven-bound lasagna. Just in time, we fled down the hill from the Resort with Craig Heath at the wheel and arrived at the Ryan kitchen to find a golden lasagna ready for eating with an accompaniment of tossed salad vinaigrette, Chateau Neuf du Pape and Central Bakery hard-crusted bread imported from Portland, Oregon. Here's how:

Serves six

8 to 12 lasagna strips (I am assuming you will use dry pasta)
1/4 lb. ground pork
1/4 lb. cooked boneless chicken breast, ground
1/4 lb. ground veal (it comes in a tube; ask your butcher)
2 cans (14.5-oz.) diced tomatoes
4 cloves garlic, peeled
1 onion
1/2 carrot
1 to 2 tbsp. dried oregano

2 tbsp. dried parsley
4 to 5 tbsp. olive oil, divided
4 tbsp. butter
3 to 4 tbsp. flour
2 cups milk
Salt and pepper to taste
1 pinch nutmeg
Mozzarella, enough to cover 3 layers (the real, wet kind is better, but use any kind that is available)
Basil, at least 1/2 cup fresh

Preheat oven to 325°.

Pyrex rectangular dish, large enough to permit 3 to 4 lasagna strips to rest on the bottom of the dish

Put in Cuisinart or other grinder garlic, onion, carrot, oregano, and parsley. Blend together. Transfer to fry pan with 2 to 3 tbsp. of olive oil in pan. Place on low heat, stir, and cook three to five minutes, then add diced tomatoes. Raise heat under pan to boil, then reduce to simmer, stirring from time to time and adding warm water to keep from thickening too much. Cook 1 to 2 hours. Then cool to warm and return to Cuisinart or blender for one to two minutes (pulse until smooth), and then return to pan.

Separately in the Cuisinart, blend pork, veal, and chicken. When ground together, cook in pan with 2 tbsp. of olive oil over low heat. Do not brown. Add salt and pepper, stirring to break up meat into a smooth mixture. Add this mixture to the tomato sauce after it has been blended and returned to its pan. Heat again to boil, then reduce to simmer and cook for about 1/2 to 1 hour. Add water to moisten, if needed.

While tomato-meat sauce simmers, prepare a béchamel (white sauce): 4 tbsp. of butter and 3 tbsp. of flour in a saucepan over low heat, stirring to blend. Then add slowly 1 to 2 cups of warmed milk, and blend by stirring.

Add salt and pepper and a grate or pinch of nutmeg. Keep warm.

In a large pan, boil water and place 12 lasagna strips in water to soften. When just limp, remove to buttered Pyrex dish, fitting lasagna strips lengthwise on bottom of dish, and cover with tomato-meat mixture; then cover with béchamel and put Mozzarella on top. Then another layer of the pasta, and repeat the process as with the first layer with another layer of pasta and cover this with slices of cheese. Dot with butter and sprinkle parsley on top. Place in oven. After 20 minutes, reduce heat to 250° and cook until top starts to turn golden. It will be bubbling and will be ready to serve.

Accompaniments

Serve with mixed green salad with a vinaigrette of white wine vinegar, garlic powder, a sprinkle of dried oregano and parsley, salt, pepper, and a squeeze of lemon, all blended with olive oil. Vinegar and oil 1/3 to 2/3. More vinegar will increase tartness. Then soften with 1/4 tsp. of sugar.

Serve with crunchy Italian or French bread.

Wine

A good Rhône, Chianti, Zonata Vallopolicella or Masi, all would be good. Since the Heaths had traveled far to risk our board, we had the Chateau Neuf du Pape. We had saved a Neppozzano Chianti Reserva for them as well, but that went the night before to accompany a Chicken Provençal with artichoke hearts, shallots, etc.

Pasta with Cherry Tomatoes and Cheese

Serves two

3 tbsp. Mozzarella cheese, cut into small pieces
4 to 5 tbsp. Monterey Jack, cut into small pieces
4 tbsp. olive oil, divided
1/2 stick butter
6 to 8 leaves fresh basil, cut with scissors
1 tbsp. dried parsley, or 1/4 cup fresh
1 clove garlic, minced
1 tbsp. oregano
Salt
Ground pepper
4 to 5 fresh cherry tomatoes
2 servings or better capellini
2 qts. water with 1 tsp. of salt to boil pasta
1/2 cup milk

Put water in medium sauce pan on high with 1 tsp. of salt to boil for cooking pasta.

Place in saucepan the cut-up stick of butter with 2 tbsp. of olive oil to heat at medium until liquefied. Stir with wooden spoon. Add cheese by bits and pieces at lowered heat; stir in one direction to emulsify. Add milk to thin the sauce.

Put pasta in boiling water. When it boils again, reduce to medium heat.

Slice tomatoes into quarters and roughly chop again. Put into second saucepan with 1 tbsp. of olive oil, garlic, salt, pepper, basil, parsley, and oregano. Stir. Cook for two to four minutes. Shift pan off stove. Avoid cooking too long

— tomatoes should not overcook.

Drain pasta, leaving some cooking water in pasta pot. Stir cheese-oil into pasta. If it does not separate, use two forks to separate and mix cheese with hot pasta. Empty contents of tomato mix into pasta, salt and pepper to taste, toss with forks, and serve. Garnish with a sprinkle of dry or fresh parsley.

Pasta with Meat Sauce

My friend Joe Bianco, who has taught me much about cooking Italian, calls this sauce a "gravy." It is also called a "ragu." For the authentic Italian method, I refer you to Joe's Cooking Italian, which is his new cookbook that preserves the recipes from his mother's native Avellino in the Compagna.

What follows is a ragu with an Irish inflection — forgive me, Joe.

Ginney, early in our courtship, said she had a longing for pasta with tomato sauce and ground beef. This is the recipe that evolved, and she gives it her enthusiastic "Okay."

Serves two

1 can (14.5-oz.) whole or diced tomatoes
1 can (8-oz.) tomato sauce (optional)
1 can (8-oz.) mushroom stems and pieces; or 6 to 8 fresh, whole mushrooms, sliced
1 to 2 yellow onions, sliced into rings and broken up in pan
2 to 3 cloves garlic, peeled and finely cut
2 tbsp. dried oregano
2 tbsp. dried parsley or 1/2 cup fresh parsley
1/2 cup fresh basil (trim with scissors into leaves), or 2 tbsp. dried basil
1/2 cup dry sherry, dry vermouth, dry white wine, or dry red wine (all optional)
1 tsp. salt
1 tsp. ground pepper
4 to 6 oz. ground beef
1 bay leaf
3 tbsp. olive oil
1 tbsp. beef base

Two frying pans are used, one to brown the ground beef and one for cooking the sauce. Use 1-1/2 tbsp. of olive oil in each pan.

At low heat, sauté garlic and onion until limp.

Blend tomatoes, herbs (except bay leaf), salt, and pepper in a food processor. Then combine with garlic and onion in saucepan, adding 1/2 tbsp. of beef base, bay leaf, and mushrooms. (If using fresh, sliced mushrooms, add them midway through cooking.)

Meanwhile, in separate pan, add 1 tbsp. of oil and crumble beef into pan. Sauté at moderate heat until color turns, then combine with tomatoes, onion, and garlic in their pan. Add wine or water to thin, if needed.

Cooking time: one-half hour to one hour (longer simmering will enhance flavor).

Serve over capellini or other pasta.

Tip: Make extra sauce and freeze for future meals.

Pork

Black Forest Ham, Scalloped Potatoes, and Spinach with Lemon and Olive Oil

September 26, 1996, Gearhart-by-the-Sea: Warm, clear days, starry night with full moon. We watch the garden from the kitchen window. My sous chef says that we have three things available for dinner — beef filets, lamb chops or a Black Forest ham. After consultation, we decided on the ham. Scalloped potatoes and lemoned spinach completed our choice. The mustard-butter-brown sugar-sherry sauce tastes good with any ham dish.

Ham

We had a Black Forest ham that required slicing, but any ham will do, including ham steaks or precooked ham. One-eighth-inch slices are about right, but thicker ones will do. Cut a slice for each portion.

Sauce

2 tbsp. butter
3 to 4 tbsp. brown sugar
2 to 3 oz. dry sherry
2 tbsp. Dijon or other mustard

Potatoes

2 to 3 baking potatoes, peeled and sliced crosswise, 1/8 inch
1 yellow onion, thinly sliced
1 clove garlic, finely chopped
1 tbsp. butter

1 tbsp. dried parsley
1/4 cup milk
Mozzarella, sufficient to cover each layer
Parmesan to cover top layer (use sliced cheese or crumbled kind) (Gruyère, Monterey Jack or other cheese may be substituted)

Spinach

Enough spinach for the number of portions — drain and press water from spinach after cooking, then add 1/4 tbsp. of olive oil and a squeeze of lemon

Order of Cooking

1. Prepare scalloped potatoes and place in preheated oven at 350°; cooking time is approximately 40 minutes.
2. Prepare sauce in a pan.
3. Slice ham about 1/8 inch. Place in a roasting pan or Pyrex dish and cook in the same oven with the potatoes.
4. Prepare the spinach.

Preparing the Scalloped Potatoes

Preheat oven to 350°.

Peel one or two baking potatoes and slice them crosswise to 1/8-inch slices. Butter a casserole dish and rub with a garlic clove on the bottom and sides, then chop the garlic finely and save it to sprinkle on the potatoes as you tier them in the casserole. Slice a yellow onion thinly. Place the potatoes neatly on the bottom of the casserole to make a first layer; cover with sliced onions, some diced fresh parsley or dried parsley, salt and pepper and a liberal sprinkling of Parmesan, slices of Mozzarella or one of the other cheeses (classic French cooking calls for Gruyère). Add a little of the remaining garlic and repeat the layers two or three times, then cover the top with a good quantity of cheese and dot the cheese with butter.

Meanwhile, heat 1/4 cup of milk and pour into each end of the casserole, taking care not to disturb the cheese topping. Place in oven. Cook for 40 minutes or until golden on top.

Check to see that the topping is golden and the liquid is well absorbed, and with the tines of a fork determine that the potatoes are cooked through.

Sauce for the Ham

Put 3 to 4 tbsp. of brown sugar in a pan with 2 tbsp. of butter. Melt the butter and liquefy the brown sugar at low heat. Add generous spurts of liquid mustard (the hot dog kind) or 2 tbsp. of Dijon. Add enough dry sherry to further liquefy the brown sugar and mustard. Cook at medium heat and stir until mixture is liquid and drips off a spoon. Watch the heat so it does not burn or overcook.

Pour over ham in a roasting pan and put the pan in the oven with the potatoes separately in their Pyrex dish. Depending on size, it should be done in less than 1/2 hour. Keep basting the ham with the sauce and add sherry to keep in the proper consistency. It should slowly drip off a spoon.

Preparing the Spinach

Place the spinach in a pan of boiling water (just about an inch) and let it steam, cooking for three to four minutes. Drain and press the spinach to remove water. Add 1/2 tbsp. of olive oil and a generous squeeze of lemon. Salt and pepper the spinach. A pinch of nutmeg is an option.

To Serve

Place ham slice on a plate and cover with sauce (make more if pan sauce is not sufficient); remove the potatoes to the plate with the crusty topping up and the spinach on the side of the plate.

Wine

We found a red Bordeaux to go with this. A Columbia Crest Chardonnay makes a tasty alternative.

Leftovers

The remaining ham is good for sandwiches, or better yet, try this, as we did the next day:

Thinly slice the cold ham. Place Romaine lettuce leaves on a plate with ham to the side. Slice tomatoes and put on the leaves and top with a thin slice of red onion. Cover with vinaigrette made with 1 tsp. of dried oregano, 1 tsp. of dried parsley, and 1 tsp. of garlic powder. Macerate and add 2 tbsp. of white wine vinegar, 2 tbsp. of olive oil, a squeeze of lemon, and a pinch of sugar, salt and pepper. Use a jar to shake, or emulsify by whisking with a spoon. Pour on the tomatoes and lettuce. Add fresh basil leaves from a pot on a sunny window sill in the kitchen. Try growing one. Fresh basil with Mozzarella is the true Italianate touch. This is also very good in soups and marinara sauce.

Wine

Try what's left of last night's wine, or a Houge Cellars Dry Semillon.

Be happy with the blessing of good food.

Ham with Juniper Berries and White Wine

We harvest juniper berries at Babs and Shep Wilson's house at Tumalo on the picturesque irrigation canal. Babs is an excellent and venturesome cook. Juniper berries are also added to sauerkraut, pork and game dishes. They are also good with an ounce of gin flambéed on elk or venison.

Serves two

1 lb. sliced ham
1 tsp. juniper berries (5 to 8 berries)
1 tsp. black peppercorns
1/4 cup white wine vinegar
1 cup dry white wine or dry vermouth
3 tbsp. butter
3 medium shallots or scallions, finely chopped
2 tbsp. flour
1 cup veal or chicken stock
2 tbsp. tomato sauce
3 to 4 tbsp. heavy cream
Salt and pepper

Preheat oven to 350°.

Put juniper berries and peppercorns in a plastic bag and crush them thoroughly with a heavy pan or rolling pin. Put the crushed spices in a saucepan, add vinegar, and cook until reduced by half (3 to 5 minutes). Add the wine and boil until reduced again by half (7 to 10 minutes). Strain sauce and reserve.

Meanwhile, melt the butter in a saucepan, add the shallots or scallions and sauté at low or medium heat until soft but not brown, two to three minutes. Stir in the flour and cook until it begins to foam; whisk in the heated stock and boil. Add the reserved sauce, whisking constantly until the sauce thickens. Add the reduced wine/juniper mixture and stir in the tomato puree, cream, salt, and pepper. Bring the sauce to a boil, then reduce to simmer, taste and adjust seasoning.

Pour a layer of sauce into a baking dish. Arrange the ham slices on top and coat them with the remaining sauce. Bake until very hot and bubbly around the edges, ten to 15 minutes. Serve the ham hot.

Pork Chops with Garlic Powder and Dry Sherry

Serves two

One pork chop per person. (I like a thin chop with some bone in. Loin chops will also do well for this dish.) Add dry oregano and parsley, as needed.
1 to 2 tbsp. olive oil
Salt and pepper
Garlic powder
1/2 tbsp. dried oregano
1/2 tbsp. dried parsley
2 to 3 oz. dry sherry
2 to 3 tbsp. butter
1 to 2 tbsp. orange marmalade, plum marmalade or orange juice, or 2 tbsp. of brown sugar to stir into sauce after deglazing pan with dry sherry (see directions below)
3 tbsp. Worcestershire sauce

Dry the pork chops and sprinkle with garlic powder, salt, pepper, dry oregano and parsley. Press mixture into chops with your fingers. Pour olive oil in fry pan, and when hot, put chops in pan. Turn when brown and cook other side. Test the chops, and when medium done, remove to a plate to keep warm.

Remove the pan from the heat and deglaze with dry sherry. Add Worcestershire sauce and a tablespoon of butter; swirl in pan and then add either orange marmalade or plum marmalade, or a good splash of orange juice, then cook down, adding sherry or butter or both as needed. Two tbsp. of brown sugar is also good, if you wish to try it as an alternative.

Pour sauce over chops when serving.

Accompaniments

Cabbage boiled in milk and water

Mashed potatoes

Slice a head of white cabbage and place it in a pan, salt and pepper it and add 1/2 water, 1/2 milk to cabbage and bring to boil, then down to simmer.

Slice 1 or 2 baking potatoes into 1/4-inch slices in water and boil until tender. Drain potatoes, adding 1/8 stick of butter and 1/4 cup of warmed milk (more or less — avoid watery potatoes). Mash thoroughly. When potatoes are well mashed and fluffy, place them on a plate with a serving of cabbage and a pork chop covered with sauce.

Pork Roast

The first of these pork roast recipes was prepared for our dear friends Dave and Lynn Templeton at our Colony Drive home in September 2000. The second was from the oven at Circulo Aguilar in Rio Rico, Arizona, for our Dutch-Canadian friend Paul Van Leuvann just before he was to leave for Montreal to join his wife, Angilina, who hies from the Dominican Republic. All of this added an international flavor to our culinary plans. These recipes differ primarily in the use of marinades and vegetable garnish. Here is the first, which has a garlic, oregano, parsley, and bay leaf rub.

Serves four

1 3- to 4-lb. pork loin roast
2 carrots, thinly sliced
1/2 onion, thinly sliced
2 whole onions, peeled and quartered
1 tbsp. dried oregano
1 bay leaf
2 to 3 tbsp. olive oil
Ground pepper
Salt
1 cup chicken stock or bouillon
1/2 cup dry sherry
2 tbsp. flour or cornstarch
2 tbsp. lemon juice
2 tbsp. Dijon mustard

Preheat oven to 325°.

Salt and pepper the roast, then spread the sliced carrots and onions in a roasting pan, leaving a bare space in the pan for the roast, with the vegetables to the side. Use a frying pan to brown the roast in 1 to 2 tbsp. of olive oil, then remove the roast to the roasting pan.

Mix garlic, oregano, olive oil, and tsp. of lemon juice, salt, and pepper, and macerate with the bottom of a soup spoon or pestle. Coat the roast with the mixture, pressing it into the roast. Add chicken stock, dried parsley and bay leaf. Put it in oven to roast. Add 3 to 4 oz. of dry sherry to the pan and baste with juices every 15 to 20 minutes. Cover the roast with a lid or foil. Covering the roast will keep it moist and is preferable to open roasting for pork. This does not apply to other types of meat. When the roast has been cooking for about 20 minutes, place the quartered onions in the pan. Add more stock, if needed; it will be the basis for the sauce to accompany the roast.

The roast is done when cooked for 35 minutes per pound or when a meat thermometer reads 180°F. When done, remove the roast onions to a plate to warm, together with the roast, covered in foil. Strain remaining jus and vegetables through a sieve into a saucepan, pressing on the vegetables to get the full flavor. Discard what is left in the sieve. Heat the jus, adding chicken stock; 2 oz. dry sherry; flour or cornstarch mixed in warm water, together with a squeeze of lemon; and Dijon mustard. Stir with wooden spoon and reduce to thickness so that sauce drips from the spoon.

Accompaniments

Roast onions

Cabbage cooked in 1/2 milk, 1/2 water, salt, and pepper

Slice the meat and serve with mashed potatoes, drained cabbage, and quartered onions. Spoon sauce over the sliced roast and sprinkle mashed potatoes with dried parsley for garnish.

Pork Roast with Marinade

As an option and following the above cooking directions, omit the oregano-garlic mix. Instead, prepare a marinade as follows:

1/2 tbsp. garlic powder
6 allspice berries, crushed
A few gratings nutmeg, or 1/4 tsp. dried nutmeg
3 to 4 whole cloves, or 1/2 tsp. cloves
1 tsp. mace
1/2 tsp. ground cinnamon
1 tbsp. dried oregano
1 tbsp. olive oil
1 tbsp. lemon juice
1 tbsp. white wine vinegar

Mix the above ingredients, macerating the herbs with the bottom of a tablespoon or a pestle. When this is done, coat the meat with it. Use a Pyrex or other dish to marinate the meat, turning it several times. Keep it in the refrigerator; one to two hours of marinating should be sufficient. Then roast as in the recipe above. Before placing the meat in the roasting pan, remove the marinade with a paper towel and dry the roast. Proceed as in the recipe above; omit the cabbage if you choose. Roast with quartered onions, carrots and roast potatoes. Roast the potatoes separately in a Pyrex or other roasting pan, or roast them with the meat, browning them first in oil in a frying pan. Prepare the mustard sauce as above. Be adequate with the sauce; our guests asked for seconds, which always pleases this cook.

Wine

Let your taste tell you what wine best goes with pork. Since Alsace is famous for its pork, Alsatian Pinot Blanc, Riesling or Gewurtztramaimer are suggestions. California, Oregon, and Washington all produce Gewurtztraminers at reasonable prices. Hogue Cellars; Flynn Vineyards; Dalles, Oregon are all good. Try a Beaujolais or a Girodas from the Rhône, if you favor the reds.

Spare Meat Patties — Chicken and Pork

I boned two chicken breasts to serve lunch to my good friend, Don Buss, on my return to Portland from Rio Rico, arizona, in December 2001. This left two chicken breast bones with some nice meat on them. I also had one pork chop with bone in the freezer. What follows is the meal I made of these.

Serves two

2 chicken breasts, strip off all meat, or two boneless breasts
1 pork chop, strip all meat from bone.
1/2 onion, sliced and chopped.
2 cloves garlic, chopped
1/2 tsp. sage, dry
1 tbsp. oregano, dry
1 tbsp. parsley, dry
3 to 4 scrapings nutmeg
3 to 4 grinds black pepper
1/2 tsp. salt
1 egg yolk
1 cup flour for dusting meat patty
2 small baby carrots
4 tbsp. olive oil

Place all ingredients except flour and egg in food processor, pulse until smooth. Remove to mixing bowl. Break egg and add yolk, mix with fingers until well mixed. On plate make two patties, about 1/4" thick and mold to form. Put 1 tbsp. oil in each of two pans, heat to sizzle.

Flour each patty on top and with flat spatula place flour side down in hot oil. Reduce heat to moderate-low. Salt and pepper and flour the face up sides, and press in flour. Watch underside to cook to golden, then turn being careful not to break up patty. Cook until cooked through, 4 to 5 minutes a side.

Meanwhile put pork and chicken bones in water with onion slices. Cook, adding water as needed. Use this as broth for sauce. When done, remove patties to serving plates in oven at warm.

Make a bèchamel with butter, flour, 1/2 cup milk, nutmeg, salt and pepper. Add about a cup of the broth and a tsp. chicken base. Cook 3 to 4 minutes. Stir and place on serving plate, placing patty on top and dribble some on top of patty with a sprinkle of dry parsley for garnish.

Accompaniments

Serve with string beans rolled in olive oil, salt, pepper and 2 shakes of garlic powder and mashed potatoes.

Pork Chops Achiote

Jeff Clock, sous-chef at Rio Rico Resort, introduced us to achiote powder. Ask for it at a Mexican grocery.

Serves two

1 tsp. achiote powder
3 tbsp. olive oil
Salt to taste
1 cup orange juice
2 loin pork chops
1 small clove garlic, finely chopped
1 tbsp. dried parsley

In Pyrex dish mix oil, achiote powder and orange juice. Place chops in marinade for 1/2 to 1 hour.

Preheat oven to 325°.

Sprinkle chops with chopped garlic and dried parsley. Place in oven and cook 45 minutes to 1 hour, basting frequently.

Accompaniments

Serve with scalloped potatoes and acorn squash with butter and brown sugar.

Poultry and Game Birds

Breaded Chicken Breasts with Artichoke-Mushroom-Cheese Sauce Lasagna

Serves two

Cheese Sauce and Pasta

2 chicken breasts, skinless and boneless
1 cup bread crumbs (Panko preferred)
1 egg (beat with fork for coating
3 tbsp. flour
1 small jar button mushrooms
Marinated artichokes with marinade oil
1 shallot, finely minced
4 green onions, finely sliced
3 tbsp. olive oil
1 tbsp. butter
1 tbsp. dried parsley
1/4 cup dry sherry
Beurre manié (1 tbsp. flour and 1 tbsp. butter, worked together with fork or fingers)
3 to 4 slices Mozzarella cheese
1 cup chicken stock or bouillon
4 leaves dry lasagna
Salt and pepper
1 small jar pimientos for garnish on chicken

Chop and mince one shallot and slice three green onions. Place in saucepan with 1 tbsp. of olive oil and a pat of butter. Cook at low heat, stirring with a wooden spoon until melted. Add one jar of marinated artichokes with marinade to sauce. Add drained contents of a small jar of button mushrooms and a grind of pepper.

In microwave, heat 1 cup of chicken stock or broth and add to sauce. Heat and stir. Make the beurre manié in a cup or bowl, melding flour and butter. Add bit by bit, stirring to thicken the sauce. Add dry sherry, then slice and crumble three to four slices of Mozzarella and stir into sauce. Add 1 tbsp. of dried parsley. Cook, stirring, until cheese melts. Keep warm.

Cook lasagna slices in flat pan in salted water to cover. Keep covered. Cook to just limp. Put two slices side by side on each plate. Spoon sauce on half of both slices; fold over and add sauce to top of slices. Garnish chicken with pimiento slices.

Preparing and Cooking Breaded Chicken Breasts

Pat dry two skinless, boneless chicken breasts, salt and pepper them, and lightly sprinkle with garlic powder. Dip in flour. Shake them in bowl with one egg stirred with a fork, then in a plate of bread crumbs.

Put 2 tbsp. of olive oil in a sauté pan. Heat at high 1 to 2 minutes then reduce to medium. Place breasts in pan. Use flat spatula to turn (watch bottom of chicken breast — do not burn). Cook to golden; turn and cook again to golden (lift side of chicken breast to see if it gets golden). Then turn down heat further to cook. It should be cooked in 20 to 30 minutes; check with tines of fork for doneness.

Accompaniments

Serve with broccoli.

Broiled Chicken

Serves two

1 2 1/2 to 3-lb. fryer, split in half with backbone removed
1 tbsp. olive oil
1 clove garlic, finely chopped
Juice of 1 lemon
2 tsp. Worcestershire sauce
1 tbsp. butter
Salt and pepper

Preheat broiler and have rack at 6 inches.

Split chicken in half. Remove breast bone. Place between sheets of wax paper and flatten with your hands or a heavy pan. With your fingers, push chopped garlic under the skin. Force your fingers through the fascia or thin membrane. Salt and pepper.

Mix oil, lemon juice, and Worcestershire sauce in bowl with salt and pepper, then brush it on both sides of chicken.

Put in a roasting pan and place in broiler. Cook skin side down for ten minutes; turn to skin side up for 15 to 20 minutes. Baste frequently. Check with tines of fork for doneness. When fluid is yellow, bird is done. Cooking time: 30 to 40 minutes.

Remove chicken and deglaze pan with 1/2 cup of chicken stock. Scrape pan and add 1 tbsp. of butter (1 tbsp. of dry sherry, optional).

Accompaniments

Serve with sauce, string beans and rice.

Chicken À la King

This is an old standby: Leftover chicken, cut into pieces and transformed into a delicacy, served on toast points or over rice.

Use chicken breasts or other parts poached at simmer to get the chicken prepared for slicing into bite-sized chunks. If you have leftover chicken, use it and skip the poaching.

Preparing Chicken

2 cups of chicken broth or stock
Salt and pepper

Place stock in pan — salt and pepper to taste and cook chicken breast or other parts at simmer. Boneless breasts are best, since they slice easily. When broth boils, turn down to simmer. After 20 minutes, test chicken with fork for doneness. Remove to plate, reserving broth. As meat cools, slice it into bite-sized pieces.

If you are using leftover chicken, cut it up and heat it in the broth. Do not do more than heat up the cooked chicken. Do not overcook; keep it tender.

Serves two

2 cups chicken, cut in bite sized pieces
2 cups chicken broth

Pepper
Salt (taste broth — it may be salty enough)
1/4 tsp. ground black pepper
1 small jar pimientos
1/2 onion, minced
1 can small bits and pieces of mushrooms (optional)
2 toast points or 1 cup rice
1 tbsp. butter
1 tbsp. flour
1/2 cup milk or cream
1 cup frozen peas
2 oz. dry sherry
2 sprinkles dry parsley

Place minced onion in saucepan with butter at medium heat, then turn down to moderate or low. Stir and let cook until limp. Be sure not to brown or burn.

Heat 2 cups of broth in another pan, add cut-up chicken pieces in pan to heat, then remove with slotted spoon to plate. Cook about five minutes at simmer. Reserve broth.

Add 1 tbsp. of flour to the saucepan butter and stir with wooden spoon until it melds. Add milk or cream, then add 1/2 cup of broth to sauce and 1 oz. of dry sherry. Cook until it thickens, then add remainder of broth. Pour cooked sauce (stir three to five minutes) into broth pan, pouring mixture in at low heat. Add pimientos and optional mushrooms, then add meat to pan and heat to serve. Before serving, add 1 cup of frozen peas. Let them heat for 3 to 4 minutes. Stir and serve over rice or on toast points.

Rice

1 cup rice
1 1/2 cups water

1 tsp. salt

Heat to boil, reduce and cover pan. Cook 10 to 15 minutes.

Toast Points

4 slices toasted sandwich bread

Slice off crust edges before toasting. Toast just to light brown. Place full slice on plate. Slice, diagonally, second slice and match to each side of slice on plate.

Serve with sprinkles of dried or minced parsley.

Wine

A Sauvignon Blanc or Chardonnay, or a red if that is your choice.

Fit for a king and filled with fond childhood memories.

Chicken À la Rio Rico

Serves four

4 chicken breasts
4 to 5 carrots (scrape and cut into 1/4-inch pieces — cut down and split thicker pieces)
2 yellow onions, cut in half and then into quarters
3 stalks celery, cut into 1-inch pieces
2 to 3 cloves garlic, chopped fine
2 to 3 oz. dry sherry (Christian Brothers or Fairbanks — Christian Brothers preferred!!)
2 to 3 tbsp. parsley (dried okay)
3/4 cup chicken stock
2 tbsp. olive oil
2 baking potatoes, peeled and sliced crosswise into 1/4-inch slices
3 to 4 tbsp. butter
2 to 3 tbsp. flour

Potatoes

Preheat oven to 350°.

Slice potatoes and place in Pyrex pan, salt and pepper, and coat with oil. Sprinkle with a small amount of chopped garlic. Then sprinkle with dried parsley. Place in oven.

Carrots and celery

Place carrots and celery in a pan of water (1/2 cup); no need to cover. Add two to three thin slices of onion with salt and pepper. Carrots and celery will be added later to chicken baking pan.

Chicken

Place olive oil in sauté pan at moderate heat.

Before placing chicken breasts in pan, dry them off with paper towels. With your fingers, place chopped garlic under skin, then salt and pepper. When olive oil is sizzling, add chicken breasts, skin side down. Brown the breasts in the pan until golden brown. Then turn and brown other side of breasts. Add quartered onions to pan and sauté and brown as breasts are browning.

Place sautéed, browned chicken in roasting pan, sprinkle with dry parsley, and put in oven. Do not cover. With fork, check carrots, and when part cooked, with a slotted spoon add carrots/celery to chicken pan. Also, add some cooking water to pan — baste chicken with sherry and juices and return to oven.

Remove potatoes (test with a fork) when done and cover to keep warm.

Cook chicken 45 minutes to 1 hour. When chicken is done (check with tines of fork), remove cooked breasts to a warm plate and cover; with a slotted spoon, remove the vegetables to another plate, and cover. When all the vegetables are on the plate, pour the juices from the plate back into the pan.

Sauce

In saucepan, melt 3 to 4 tbsp. of butter and 2 to 3 tbsp. of flour on low heat; mix with a wooden spoon. Add chicken stock to thin out roux, stirring. Then strain sauce from chicken pan, slowly stirring. Add a splash or two of dry sherry, keep cooking, check for taste, and cook until it drops from spoon and is slightly thick.

Put sauce on plate first, then chicken, vegetables, and potatoes on top of sauce.

Chicken Bordelaise

Serves four

1 2 1/2 to 3 lb. frying chicken, cut up
3 tbsp. butter
3 tbsp. olive oil or vegetable oil
16 to 24 whole, peeled shallots, or 16 1-inch peeled white onions, or 1 yellow onion chopped
1 tsp. salt
Freshly ground pepper, to taste
2 bay leaves
1 tsp. lemon juice
1 9-oz. package frozen artichoke hearts, defrosted and drained (see below for alternative, using 1 jar of marinated artichoke hearts)
1/2 cup of chicken stock

Preheat oven to 350°.

Wash chicken under cold water, then dry thoroughly. Damp chicken won't brown well, and we want golden parts. In fry pan, melt butter and oil at moderate heat, place chicken skin side down, and cook until golden. Turn and brown other side. Remove chicken when golden to plate; continue browning until all chicken is browned. Sauté shallots or onions in pan until golden, then return chicken to pan with shallots. Add 1/2 cup of chicken stock and two bay leaves. Cook in oven for 30 to 40 minutes.

In a separate pan, heat 1 tbsp. of butter and 1 tbsp. of oil, and when butter foams, put in artichokes and lemon juice, and sauté. Shake in pan for about five minutes. This version is our favorite.

Serve with a pasta.

Alternative

Instead of frozen artichokes, add a jar of marinated hearts together with marinade. Pour over chicken and cook with chicken about 15 minutes before chicken is done.

Chicken Marengo

The dish described below is not a classic "Marengo." The legend of its origin goes something like this (the details, like the recipe, being partially forgotten at this writing): Napoleon in his Italian campaign was to face the Austrians at this northern Italian village. His chef was hard put to find any suitable viands for the young general's dinner. He came up with "Chicken Marengo." It used to be served at Eric Ladd's Kamm House restaurant in the 50s and was served by "Ike," formerly the major domo at the old Portland Hotel. A fried egg was part of the classic Marengo, sort of like the egg on a true Wiener Schnitzel. Enough of history! This is what I cooked at Virginia's request:

Serves four

3-1/2 to 4 lbs. whole chicken, disjointed, or use selected parts of chicken — simmer neck in pan of water with slice of onion for stock
2 to 3 tbsp. olive oil
Salt and pepper to taste
5 to 6 mushrooms, sliced
3 cloves garlic, finely chopped
1 yellow onion, thinly sliced, or 3 to 4 shallots, sliced
1 cup dry sherry to taste, or white wine
Chicken broth or chicken base in water or stock, as directed below
1 can (14-oz.) diced tomatoes
1 tbsp. oregano
1 tbsp. parsley

Pour olive oil in a Dutch oven or frying pan placed on stove at medium heat. Reduce heat and place chicken in pan skin side down after drying with paper towel and sprinkling with salt and pepper. Remove to plate after browning. Put onion and garlic in pan with oil at low heat, stirring from time to time until garlic and onions are limp. (Break up sliced onions to rings when you place in pan.) Remove from pan to a plate and keep warm.

Add oil if needed and place chicken parts in pan skin side up. Pour juice from plate into pan, then sprinkle with oregano and parsley, together with onion (or shallots) and garlic from plate, and turn up heat. Adding 1/2 cup of chicken broth, dry sherry, and diced or crushed tomatoes. I use sherry, but a cup of dry white wine will do as well. Reduce heat, cover, and simmer with some bubbling. Cook 45 minutes to one hour on top of stove or in 350° oven.

Check with fork for tenderness. When the juice runs yellow, the chicken is done.

When done, remove chicken to flat roasting pan and briefly brown under broiler to restore color. Cook down sauce in pan to reduce if needed; thicken with cornstarch or flour if needed.

Accompaniments

Juice of 1/2 lemon to squeeze on broccoli with a splash of olive oil

Steam broccoli, drain and splash with olive oil and lemon.

Cook capellini in salted water.

Then place chicken on plates with capellini and broccoli on the side. Pour sauce over chicken and capellini. Serve.

Wine

We had a Vallopolicella (1996) Zonata. Another suggestion was a Drouhin Chardonnay from Burgundy, but the red was the first choice.

Voilà!

Chicken Poached in Butter

Serves two

2 skinless, boneless chicken breasts
4 to 5 shallots or green onions, minced in processor
Salt and pepper
1/4 stick butter
1/2 cup chicken stock
1/2 cup white wine or dry vermouth
2 tbsp. lemon juice (juice of 1/2 lemon)
1 tbsp. flour
1/2 cup cream or half and half (optional)

Chicken:

Preheat oven to 325°.

Dry and salt and pepper breasts, and place in casserole with butter cut into slices, minced shallots, and wine. Cook in oven for about 30 minutes, basting frequently. When done, turn down oven, remove chicken and onions to plate and place in warm oven while sauce is made.

Sauce:

Deglaze pan and pour into a saucepan. Add 1 tbsp. of flour and stir until melded. Add chicken stock and taste for flavor. Add a squeeze of lemon. Cook down to thickness. (Optional: Add cream or half-and-half.) Serve over chicken with rice, peas, or green beans.

Optional: Cook sliced mushrooms in stock or white wine with a squeeze of lemon juice, then add to sauce.

Chicken Tetrazzini

Serves four

3 cups cooked chicken, cut into small pieces
6 to 8 mushrooms, sliced
1/2 cup cream or half-and-half
2 to 3 oz. dry sherry
1/2 cup grated or powdered Parmesan cheese
1/4 tsp. paprika
2 portions capellini pasta
Salt and pepper
1 tbsp. dried parsley
1 carrot, chopped
1 clove garlic, diced
1 small onion, diced

Preheat oven to 325°.

If your chicken is already cooked, peel off the skin and cut it into bite-sized chunks. If it is not cooked, take two boned breasts or thighs and poach in water with salt, a little dry vermouth, and a slice of onion. When cooked, peel off skin and cut up the chicken meat. Slice mushrooms and sauté in pan with 1 tbsp. of butter and a splash of dry sherry. Boil carrots until tender and chop very fine.

Use chicken bouillon for 1 cup of broth, or use broth from poaching liquid. Put chunks of chicken in pan with broth, bring to a simmer and heat through, then add 1 to 2 jiggers of sherry.

Cook pasta in water until al dente.

Butter a bread-loaf-sized casserole and place 1/3 of the capellini on the bottom, then spread 1/2 of cooked chicken, carrots, garlic, onion , and parsley. Sprinkle with

Parmesan. Repeat process, then cover with remaining pasta and sprinkle remaining Parmesan on top. Add 1/2 cup of warmed cream and a jigger of sherry. Place in oven and cook one-half hour or until top begins to get golden. It is now ready to serve with a salad vinaigrette.

Note: leftover turkey can be substituted for chicken.

Wine

A Chardonnay, rosé or Chianti are all good choices to attend upon the chicken. Voilà!

Cornish Game Hen

This is Ginney's recipe, memorable because she cooked this for me for the first time at Knaus Road in Lake Oswego.

Serves two (requires candlelight)

1 Cornish game hen, defrosted and split in half
Salt and pepper
3 to 4 tbsp. brown sugar
1 tbsp. butter
1 tbsp. oil
1 tbsp. Worcestershire sauce
1 tsp. lemon juice
2 oz. dry sherry

Preheat broiler with rack 6 inches from heat.

Split hen, salt and pepper. In saucepan, mix brown sugar, butter, oil, Worcestershire sauce, lemon juice, and dry sherry. Heat to liquefy. Then baste hen with basting brush. Place in broiling pan skin side down. Put under broiler for 15 minutes, then baste further, turn, and cook for 20 to 30 minutes, basting frequently. Remove and strain cooking juices into gravy boat.

Accompaniments

Serve with rice and green peas.

Lemon Chicken

Dimitri, at his restaurant on West Burnside and 17th Avenue in Portland, introduced us to this dish. Since then, we have cooked it this way.

Serves two

2 chicken legs, thighs and drumsticks attached, or 2 half chickens (fryers)
4 to 5 garlic cloves, minced or finely chopped
1/2 cup lemon juice
2 to 3 tbsp. oregano, dried
Salt
1 to 2 tbsp. ground pepper
2 to 3 tbsp. dried parsley, or 1/2 cup fresh, chopped
1 baking potato, peeled and sliced crosswise in 1/8-inch slices
1/2 cup olive oil
1 cup chicken broth or bouillon

Preheat oven to 350°.

Wash and dry chicken, trimming away any pieces of loose fat. Mix the garlic, oregano, oil, lemon juice, salt, and pepper in a bowl and then rub it on chicken on both sides. Also, salt and pepper the potato slices. Put chicken in oven for 15 minutes, then place potatoes in roasting pan with chicken. Test chicken with fork after one hour of cooking. When juices run yellow, chicken is done. Sprinkle parsley on chicken and serve with potatoes from pan.

After removing chicken and potatoes from pan, deglaze the pan with some water or chicken broth, dry white wine, or dry sherry. If you wish to thicken the sauce, add 1 tbsp. of butter. Pour over chicken.

Wine

A dry Semillon, or any Graves or white Burgundy, will add to your eating pleasure. The Chardonnays also await you. Try a Sokol-Blosser from the Dundee area in Yamhill County, Oregon. Greece also offers many fine wines. I would avoid the Retsinas. Ask your wine store for help and try a Greek wine. It will be a rewarding adventure. If you live in Portland, drop by and ask Dimitri for advice.

Quail, Grilled

In southern Arizona, quail flourish. On the side of an arroyo on the margin of our yard, two coveys nested in some fruit tree prunings. They had been safe in our keeping and were gone by the time Dr. Tom Wendel arrived in February 2000 to hunt quail. After three days of uphill and downdale hunting, he rewarded us with four Gambel Quail, plucked and cleaned.

We grilled them on a B-B-Que grill over mesquite coals. (Any charcoal or your oven broiler will do.) Place the birds 4 to 6 inches below the broiler.

4 quail, cleaned and split to flatten
3 tbsp. olive oil
Salt and pepper
3 limes, juiced
1 tbsp. Worcestershire sauce
1/4 tsp. garlic powder

Partially split bird and flatten with the palms of your hands. Salt and pepper. Dry quail and baste with brush, using basting sauce made as follows: In a bowl, mix olive oil, lime juice, garlic powder and Worcestershire sauce.

After brushing quail, place on grill 4 to 6 inches above coals, bone side down. Cook ten minutes and baste again. Then turn and cook skin side down. Baste frequently. Turn when skin is crisp. Cook for another ten minutes or more.

Check for doneness by moving the leg. If it gives/moves easily, the bird is done. Also, pierce with fork; if the fluid is yellow, the bird is done.

Accompaniments

Serve with rice mixed with sliced mushrooms and 1 tbsp. of minced scallions/green onions. Sauté mushrooms and scallions with 1 tbsp. of butter plus olive oil.

As for the vegetables, we suggest green peas or beans, drained and buttered. Spinach with olive oil and lemon would be a good addition.

Roast Chicken

Serves two to four

1 3 to 4 lb. chicken
1 carrot, chopped
1 onion, chopped
1/2 cube butter
1 cup chicken broth
2 cloves garlic, finely chopped
1 baking potato, peeled and cut crosswise in 1/8-inch slices
2 tbsp. olive oil
2 cups frozen peas
2 oz. dry sherry

Preheat oven to 350°.

Clean roasting chicken under cold water and dry with paper towels. If available, remove neck and put in pan with 2 cups of water; three slices of onion; a small carrot, diced; salt; and pepper. Add loose fat trimmings, if any, to cook in broth. Otherwise, make broth with 1 tbsp. of chicken base and 1 cup of water.

Salt and pepper outside of chicken and inside of cavity. Put your fingers under the skin over breast and push the chopped garlic under the skin of the breast. Don't be afraid to push fingers through the fascia if it seems to get in your way. Rub outside of chicken with butter and put about 1 tbsp. of butter in cavity.

Pour 1 tbsp. of Wesson or olive oil in roasting pan and scatter chopped onion and carrots in pan. Place chicken in pan breast up. Put in oven. When breast begins to brown to a golden hue, turn it on its side for another ten minutes, and then, with breast down, for ten minutes, and return it to breast up position. Baste frequently with pan juices. After one-half hour, reduce oven to 325°. Check with the tines of a large fork at the leg. If fluid is yellow, chicken is done. Remove chicken to warming platter, turn oven off, and then place chicken in oven to keep warm.

With slotted spoon, remove onion-carrot mix from juice in pan and press it with another spoon to get all juice in pan, and then discard. Use paper towel or bulb to degrease juices. Some will remain, which is good. Pour dry sherry or white wine into sauce and add broth, continuing to heat juices and reduce them to desired thickness, stirring with a wooden spoon. Carve chicken to serving plates and pour sauce over chicken. Pour the remainder of sauce on the plate and place roast potatoes and peas on top of sauce.

When you put the chicken in the oven, prepare the potatoes and peas as follows:

Roast Potatoes

Put 2 tbsp. of olive oil in Pyrex or other roasting pan, add potato slices, laying them flat. Salt and pepper. Place in oven along with chicken. Stir with spoon with long handle so potatoes will not stick to bottom of dish. Potatoes should be done in about 40 minutes. Remove and cover pan with plate to keep warm.

Peas

When roast chicken and sauce are ready, add 2 cups of frozen peas to boiling water and reduce heat. After two to four minutes, turn up heat momentarily and remove, drain and refresh under cold water. Drain again and add 1 tbsp. of butter to pan, swirl peas in butter, and add salt and pepper. Spoon onto plate beside roast potatoes. You are now ready to marry this delightful dish to a pleasing wine.

Wine

Virginia suggests a Meridian Vineyards 1997 Chardonnay or a Houge Cellars Chenin Blanc. If you feel spendy, try a Pouilly Fuise or any white Burgundy. Dry Semillons and Sauvignon Blanc are neglected whites that do well with chicken. The Bordeaux are combinations of these two and the Graves are so often neglected in favor of the ubiquitous Chardonnay. We had this dinner with leisurely conversation on the patio as the setting sun reddened the Santa Ritas to the east. Ah, wilderness is paradise enow.

Roast Turkey With Dressing Isle of Guernsey Style

"Mike" Etheridge, my mother's good friend from the Isle of Guernsey, a British island off the coast of Normandy, gave this recipe to my mother. The following is my reconstruction from my memory of watching Mother prepare this. I would be helping by turning the handle of the old cast iron meat grinder, which was clamped to the pull-out bread board in the kitchen on 12th Street.

Stuffing

2 cups dry bread chunks
2 cups parsley, chopped
2 cups beef suet, ground
1 cup onion, chopped
1 egg
1/2 tbsp. sage, dried
2 tbsp. butter, melted
1 tbsp. oil
Salt and pepper

Grind beef suet and then sauté on low heat in 1 tbsp. of oil (suet will melt down). Reserve. In processor, coarsely pulse onion, parsley, salt, pepper, and sage. Put in mixing bowl with sautéed suet and other ingredients. Break egg into mixture and mix with hands, then fold in bread chunks. Add melted butter.

Use this stuffing for birds. Do not crowd into cavity. Any extra roast in small pan.

Turkey

Preheat oven to 325° for unstuffed, 350° for stuffed.

Clean and dry bird — stuff it as above. Truss legs with string.

Place in oven on rack. For unstuffed bird, cook 25 minutes per pound. For stuffed bird, cook 30 to 35 minutes. Baste frequently. When done, remove turkey to platter. Turn oven down to warm and return turkey to oven, and prepare gravy.

Turkey Gravy

While roasting turkey, put neck in soup pan with water to cover, salt and pepper, two slices of onion, and one-half stalk of celery. Bring to boil, then simmer to make stock.

Degrease drippings in roasting pan, over medium heat on top of stove, add 1 cup of stock. Stir bottom of pan with spoon. Add more stock for volume as needed.

Thicken gravy with 2 tbsp. of flour in 1/4 cup of warm water, mixed with spoon or shaken in jar. Turn down heat and add slowly to gravy to thicken. Add more flour-water as needed.

Accompaniments

Serve with: mashed potatoes, peas, carrots, sweet potatoes, or turnip puree (squash and turnip puree) with butter.

Chicken and Red Pepper with Sauce Mornay and Cappelini

Serves two

2 chicken breasts, cooked and cut into bite sized pieces
2 tbsp olive oil
1/2 sweet red pepper, diced small
1/2 onion, thinly sliced
2 cups chicken broth
2 tbsp. butter
2 tbsp. flour
1 cup milk
1/2 cup Monterey Jack cheese, shredded
2 servings cappelini

Put olive oil in fry pan at low heat and add onion and diced pepper, cook for 10 minutes stirring with wooden spoon. Do not brown onion. After cooking to limp add 1 cup chicken broth. Raise heat to boil then reduce to low.

In sauce pan make white sauce with flour, butter, milk and nutmeg, then add cheese to make a mornay. Add salt and pepper to taste and 1 cup chicken broth. Cook to thicken then add this to pan with onions and red pepper. Stir together and cook for 5 minutes at medium. Add chicken pieces and heat for another 10 minutes.

Serve over cappelini.

Seafood

Fish on the Oregon Coast

In the 1950s, when I had the impression that Oregon was a culinary desert or a place of limited culinary options, I happened upon an article in *Gourmet* magazine. I had lived during the war for a short time in France and had traveled elsewhere and also lived in New York, and from time to time I made culinary expeditions to San Francisco in the 1940s and 50s. San Francisco, of course, was an adventure to visit because Oregon at that time did not have liquor over the bar, and my survey of the total wine lists of Oregon restaurants found that only one served wine with dinner, and that was the famous — now gone — Henry Thiele's, which was a wonderful restaurant with mostly German-style cooking. In Thiele's they had a wine list consisting of the following: white, Concannon Vineyards Sauterne; red, Concannon Vineyards Red Burgundy.

The cooking in Oregon was great if you could find it — steaks, prime rib, fried chicken, broiled salmon, washed down with whiskey and water. So you can see, for a young fellow who had been introduced to the delights of New York, London, Paris and San Francisco, Oregon didn't seem to offer food San Francisco style. Oregon home cooking restaurants were really tasty. But the *Gourmet* article awakened me to the beauties of the food of the Oregon coast. I read it with great delight because I opened the article by reading about collecting and cooking crab; clams, particularly razor clams and steamer clams; filet of sole; halibut; and cod, all prepared in marvelous fashions. I found out that the author was not talking about Nantucket, Massachusetts; or Baltimore with its crab cakes; or Long Island with its famous oysters, but good old Gearhart, Oregon, which was a favorite place of mine. The author was not then as famous as he was to become, but he was an

Oregon native who regularly visited Gearhart and cooked at Gearhart, James Beard. So some of my recipes deal with the wonderful fish that are obtainable at the Oregon coast.

Halibut Baked with Onions and Parmesan Cheese, Vermouth and Lemon

We served this on the deck at Riverpoint in Portland while watching the sailboats circle in the Willamette. Virginia brought home about one pound of fresh halibut and requested that I prepare it as I would. This is the story of how we made this fish fit for summer eating. It will do well in the winter also, so don't confine yourself — eat it anytime.

Serves two

1 lb. halibut, cut into two serving pieces
2 tbsp. olive oil
2 tbsp. flour
Ground pepper; salt
1/2 cup yellow onions or green onions, minced
1 lemon for juice
1 tbsp. dried parsley or minced fresh
Parmesan cheese, grated or powdered, to cover fish
2 oz. dry vermouth or dry sherry
1 clove garlic, minced, or garlic powder
Capellini for two
String beans
1 patty butter

Preheat oven to 350°.

Put olive oil in casserole dish and coat the two pieces of halibut with oil. Sprinkle with salt and pepper. Squeeze lemon or pour its juice directly on fish. Be sure fish is white side up and skin on bottom.

Now put flour on fish and pat in with fingers. Spread

chopped onion over fish and around sides. Then cover fish with Parmesan cheese and liberally dot cheese with thumb-sized dots of butter. Pour on side of dish, not on top of fish, enough dry vermouth or sherry to cover bottom of dish but only part way up the top. Put several slices of the peel from the lemon into dish with other ingredients. Place in oven.

When the top begins to brown (after cooking about 15 to 20 minutes), test with fork. If fork yields, it should be done.

Then sprinkle a bit more Parmesan on top and turn up broiler until top begins to turn golden. The fish is then ready. Remove to heated plate.

Meanwhile: Take tips from string beans. Place in pot with salted water. Boil until tender. Drain and refresh under cold water. Return pot to low heat and sprinkle garlic powder with a splash of olive oil, then salt and pepper. Shake pot to coat beans with oil.

Boil pot of salted water for pasta and put in enough capellini for two. Reduce heat and cook for about six minutes or until al dente.

Sauté olive oil and minced garlic clove at low heat in frying pan. When softened, drain pasta into frying pan with a cup of pasta water to mix with oil, and be ready to serve. If it sits too long, add some more pasta water to keep it from sticking.

Serve halibut on plate over spoonful of the cooking juice, put pasta on plate together with beans. Use flat spatula to remove fish in one piece.

Wine

A Houge Cellars chenin blanc was the wine of choice — chilled, of course.

Best of dining.

Halibut Meunière

This is a French word meaning "Miller's Wife." Halibut steaks dredged in flour on a plate and then sautéed in a skillet in 1 tbsp. of butter and 1 tbsp. of oil.

Serves two

2 halibut steaks, 1 inch thick (preferably boneless)
Salt and pepper
1 tbsp. of butter
1 tbsp. of oil
1 lemon, cut in wedges
4 tbsp. of flour

Wash halibut in cold water and dry it. Place flour in plate. Salt and pepper the steaks. Lightly dredge in flour. Shake off excess flour.

Melt 1 tbsp. of butter and 1 tbsp. of oil in skillet at moderate heat. When that has melted, put the steaks in the skillet. Be sure to keep heat down to avoid burning butter and fish. Turn when golden on underside. Cook three to four minutes; cook after turning for three to four minutes. Use tines of fork to test. When they yield easily, remove fish to plate and place in oven at warm.

Accompaniments

Serve with buttered peas, mashed or baked potatoes, and lemon wedges.

Alternative: Lemon-butter sauce with capers

1/2 tbsp. lemon juice
3 tbsp. butter
1 tbsp. oil
2 tbsp. capers
Pepper
1 oz. dry white wine, dry vermouth or dry sherry (optional)

Wipe skillet clean with paper towels. Melt butter in oil. Pour in lemon juice, whip or stir butter vigorously, and add capers and a grind of pepper. Cook down to thickness. If sauce needs thickening, add a little beurre manié to give a better consistency. Pour over halibut.

If you wish, add wine and cook down sauce.

This can also be done with chilled butter whipped in pan over low heat, chunk by chunk, with lemon juice added.

Orange Roughy

This fish comes from the ocean around New Zealand. Filets come in frozen form. It is delicious. Here are the ingredients for the roughy. It is to be sautéed in 1 to 2 tbsp. of olive oil in a nonstick pan, if available.

Serves two

1 lb. orange roughy filet (defrosted)
1 tbsp. olive oil
Panko or other bread crumbs
1 cup flour
1 egg, beaten with fork
1 lemon, squeezed
1 tsp. sugar
2 tbsp. or more of butter
2 tbsp. capers
Salt and pepper
Garlic powder

Wash and dry the fish. Cut into two portions. Salt, pepper, and lightly dust fish with garlic powder. Put flour on one plate, bread crumbs on another, and the eggs in a soup plate. Stir with a fork. Dust fish with flour; dip in egg mixture, then roll in bread crumbs. Press crumbs with fingers so they adhere to filet.

Heat oil in sauté pan on medium. Place fish in pan when oil sizzles, then reduce heat to low. Use a flat plastic spatula. Watch and lift fish to see how it is cooking. Keep heat down to avoid burning. When golden, turn fish and cook other side to golden color. Test fish with fork for doneness. It should go in easily. When done (about eight minutes), remove fish to plate and put in a warming oven.

Wipe pan with paper towels, and over low heat, melt 2 tbsp. of butter in a little oil, squeeze one-half to one lemon into butter, stir to meld, and add 1/2 tsp. of sugar and 2 tbsp. of drained capers.

When mixed, place some of the sauce on a plate, put filet on top and pour remaining sauce on top.

Accompaniments

Serve with spinach and mashed potatoes.

Poached Salmon

This poaching method will give you hot or cold salmon filets.

Serves four

4 salmon filets
1 cup dry vermouth (Gallo)
1/2 cup white wine vinegar
1 sprig fresh parsley tied on string
5 to 6 peppercorns
1/2 tsp. salt
1 bay leaf
2 to 3 cups water
2 tbsp. capers
1/2 tbsp. lemon juice

Pour liquids and spices, except capers, into nonreactive fry pan. Heat to boil; reduce to simmer. Cook for five to ten minutes. Be sure liquid fills pan to cover fish, add water if needed.

Wash and dry fish; salt and pepper. Put in pan at simmer; cook for about eight minutes. Check with fork for doneness. Remove fish to plate to warm. Strain liquid through sieve. Save juice to add to sauce.

Sauce

Make roux in saucepan. Add poaching liquid to mix with roux to desired thickness. Add lemon juice. Salt and pepper to taste, then add capers. Pour over filets and serve.

You can also use Ginney's Cold Sauce.

Cold Poached Salmon

Dry and cool poached filets (place in refrigerator). Serve with Ginney's mustard mayonnaise cold sauce and cold asparagus. Garnish with parslied lemon wedge and sliced cucumbers.

Ginney's Cold Sauce
(for asparagus and salmon, hot or cold)

3 tbsp. mayonnaise (Best Foods)
2 tbsp. Dijon mustard
1 tbsp. lemon juice
2 tbsp. capers
1 tsp. caper juice

Mix all ingredients in bowl until melded. Taste to adjust ingredients. Serve on the side or dress by putting sauce over salmon and asparagus.

As a dip for cold asparagus, this also makes a delicious hors d'oeuvre.

Prawns Napoli

Imagine the Isle of Ischia and the Bay of Naples as you prepare this.

This dish is redolent of the flavors of garlic, tomatoes, oregano and basil (fresh if possible). Olive oil lends its flavor along with lemon. Fresh prawns or large shrimp are preferred, but cooked frozen shrimp make delectable eating.

Serves four

3 medium prawns per serving (12 in all), shelled and deveined
1 tbsp. oregano, dried
1 tbsp. of parsley, dried (1/2 cup fresh)
1/2 cup basil, fresh chopped (1 tbsp. dried)
1 can (14.5 oz.) diced tomatoes
Salt and ground pepper
1 cup dry white wine, dry vermouth, or sherry
Capellini, for four
1 yellow onion, thinly sliced
3 cloves garlic, peeled and minced
4 tbsp. olive oil, divided
1/2 lemon, squeezed
1 tbsp. butter

Shell and devein fresh prawns. In hot fry pan. place 2 tbsp. of olive oil, reduce heat, and add sliced onions and garlic to pan, stirring frequently with wooden spoon. Don't brown; keep heat down, stirring until onions are limp. After five minutes, add salt and pepper to taste, tomatoes, chopped basil, oregano, and parsley, stirring to mix, and raise heat to medium; cook five to ten minutes.

In separate sauté pan, use 2 tbsp. of olive oil, and at moderate heat, sauté shrimp in oil, adding pepper; lemon juice; 1/2 cup of the wine; and at end, butter. Remove from heat after turning shrimp and shaking pan. Total cooking time: four minutes maximum. They will take on a red color. Reduce sauce if needed.

If frozen shrimp are used, shake in pan with olive oil to heat after defrosting under cold water tap. Do not cook too long.

Meanwhile, cook capellini for four in boiling, salted water for five to six minutes. Strain with server to plates. Pour sauce on capellini and top with prawns and sauce from pan. Sprinkle with parsley and serve.

Red Snapper for a Winter Evening

This is good any time of the year, but was cooked at chez Ryan at Gearhart by the Sea, where our appetites were freshened by a winter walk on the Pacific shore with a turn to follow Necanicum Bay. We turned from the bar where the Necanicum empties into the Pacific and followed the river back to the cozy cabin. Here are the fixings and how to do it:

Serves four

Red snapper, fresh, cut into four serving slices
Salt and pepper
Milk in plate to cover fish before dredging
Dredging flour
1 tbsp. white of green onion thinly sliced (two will do)
3 tbsp. butter, divided
1 lemon for juice
2 tbsp. olive oil
2 tbsp. capers, drained
Dry vermouth or any dry white wine (this can be omitted, using butter and lemon only)

Salt and pepper snapper, then turn over in milk on plate, shake and then roll in flour, shake again and they are ready for the frying pan.

In a pan with olive oil and 1 tbsp. of butter, place some thinly sliced white part of green onions. Cook at low heat until they soften. Remove to plate. Turn up heat to medium and place floured fish in pan. Cook until golden and turn with flat spatula until underside is also cooked. Use tines of fork to check for doneness. When it yields easily, remove fish to warm plate. Turn heat down in pan. Deglaze with dry vermouth and add 2 tbsp. of butter and a squeeze of lemon, together with cooked green onions and the capers. Pour over fish after placing it on serving plates, then add a sprinkle of parsley.

This same cooking method can be used with rockfish or other white fish. With sole, be sure to fry quickly, since it is a very tender fish. A lemon-butter sauce can be made in a saucepan other than the fish pan by using butter, dry vermouth, and lemon juice. If you like, thicken the sauce by adding a little flour (1 tsp.) and stir into the butter.

Accompaniments

Serve with boiled red potatoes, buttered.

To accompany this, cook spinach in pan with 1 to 2 inches of boiling water for two minutes, then drain and squeeze with slotted spoon, draining the water from the pan. Splash with olive oil and squeeze a little lemon on it.

Wine

Some wine choices: Ours was a 1996 Houge Cellars Chenin Blanc. Other good ideas: a Mouton Cadet Red or a Bordeaux Entre-Deux-Mers. This last is an old standard with fish or shellfish.

Roast Red Snapper

My sous chef, Ginney, brought back a good quantity of red snapper from the fishmonger in Seaside. She suggested I prepare something unusual. This roast version is my response. The idea was inspired by a meal I had at the kitchen of my good friend Joe Bianco of Portland, Italian chef of well-deserved repute and a true bon vivant.

Serves two

1 lb. red snapper, cut into serving sizes
1 baking potato, peeled and sliced crosswise in 1/8-inch slices
4 cloves garlic, finely chopped
Olive oil
2 carrots, peeled and cut into 1-inch slices
1 yellow onion, sliced into quarter sections
2 sprigs fresh rosemary from yard, or 1 tbsp. dried oregano
Milk in plate to coat fish before dredging with flour
Flour in plate for dredging fish
Ground pepper and salt to taste
1/2 lemon for juice
Garlic powder
2 tbsp. dried parsley
Zucchini, cut lengthwise in half, then cut into 1-inch pieces
2 oz. dry sherry (preferably Christian Brothers)
1 tomato cut in half, or 2 if desired

Preheat the oven to 350°.

Prepare the potatoes, zucchini, onion, garlic, and carrots. Peel garlic by placing knife flat on clove and, with heel of hand, hit surface. Garlic skin will then be easily removed. Then chop finely. First place the carrots and potatoes in a pan with water just to cover. Parboil these vegetables for ten minutes.

Meanwhile, add 2 tbsp. of olive oil to a Dutch oven or casserole. Place parboiled vegetables, onion quarters, zucchini, and halved tomatoes in roasting pan; sprinkle with chopped garlic. Put dried oregano and parsley on tomato with salt and pepper. Add a sprig of rosemary, salt and ground pepper or, if you prefer, a liberal sprinkling of 1 tbsp. of dried oregano. Put vegetables in oven. Cook for 20 minutes.

Dredge snapper in milk, then in flour. Sprinkle garlic powder on floured fish and salt and pepper. Remove pan from oven and place fish in bottom of pan, moving vegetables to side. Squeeze lemon on fish. Pour in dry sherry around fish. Bake 10 to 15 minutes, the fish should be cooked and ready to serve with the vegetables. Spoon out onto the plates.

White wine or dry vermouth can be substituted for the sherry; a slightly different taste will result that will also be tasty.

Arrange the fish on plate with the potatoes to the side, the tomato in the center, and the other vegetables next to the roasted potatoes. Light the candles and turn on some tango music.

Wine

We opened the wine cabinet and brought forth three wines to go with this rich dish: A Christian Moueix 1996 Merlot (Bordeaux), a Rodney Strong 1998 Sonoma County Chardonnay, and a Zenato 1998 Pinot Grigio Delle Venezie. We opted for the Pinot Grigio.

Rock Fish with Enriched White Sauce, Lemon and Capers

Rock fish, sole or flounder filets (red snapper will also do), cut into serving pieces
1/2 cup dry vermouth or dry white wine
Bay leaf
3 green onions, finely chopped
4 tbsp. flour
3/4 cup milk
3 to 4 tbsp. butter, divided
2 to 3 oz. dry sherry or white wine
2 tbsp. white wine vinegar
1/2 lemon, for juice
Green beans
1/2 tbsp. olive oil
3/4 cup shredded Mozzarella
2 tbsp. capers
Salt and pepper
Baking potatoes, cut in half lengthwise

Wash and dry filets and remove bones with pliers (feel along fish); cut into serving sizes. Use stainless steel or other nonreactive frying pan. Finely chop green onions (use white ends only but you may include some of the green where it joins the white). Put 1 tbsp. of butter in pan and then mix the onions in with the butter, cooking at moderate to low heat until soft but translucent. Do not overheat and burn. Cook three to four minutes, then add 1/4 cup of water and an equal amount of dry white wine or dry vermouth and bay leaf. Bring to boil and then reduce to simmer.

When the broth has simmered for five to ten minutes, put the fish in the pan to poach. Cover pan and cook three to four minutes, take off the cover, and test for doneness with tines of a fork. When fork penetrates easily, the fish is done. Remove fish to plate and cover to keep warm, reserving liquid..

White Sauce

In a saucepan, melt 3 tbsp. of butter at low heat and then stir in flour, making a roux. Slowly stir milk into the roux. Pour fish broth through strainer or sieve into roux and reduce by cooking at moderate heat, stirring to mix. Discard bay leaf. Add to this the dry sherry, white wine vinegar and lemon juice. Add the Mozzarella.and capers and enrich with more sherry, if needed. Cook until thickened. It should drip off a spoon.

This recipe is a variation on the sauces stemming from white sauce with juices added. The cheese is a version of the mornay. The lemon, white wine and vinegar are used in established sauces such as Bearnaise. It's fun to use the variations. Good cooking!

Green Beans

Place tipped green beans in boiling water with 1/4 tsp. of salt; cook until tender. Drain and refresh under cold water, then drain again. Sprinkle lightly with garlic powder and add 1/2 tbsp. of olive oil, heat, then cover to keep warm.

Baked Potato

Clean, brush and place in microwave for ten minutes or more. Slice in half and mash with fork with butter, ground pepper, and Lawrey's Seasoned Salt.

Serving Suggestion

Place potatoes and beans on one half of the plate with two servings of fish. Cover the fish with the sauce and serve.

Wine

We tried a Robert Mondavi Coastal Cabernet Sauvignon. Another selection: a George Drouhin Bourgone Chardonnay, 1996. A dry Semillon would do well also.

Poached Trout in White Wine with Spinach

Serves six

Stuffing

1 lb. fresh spinach, or frozen
1/2 stick butter
2 shallots, chopped
2 clove garlic, chopped
1/2 cup crème fraiche or heavy cream
1 medium bunch parsley, leaves only, chopped
1 tbsp. grated zest of lemon
1 large pinch nutmeg
Salt and pepper
2 slices stale white bread cut into pieces

Trout

12 small trout (about 2 lbs.), with skin, if trout unavailable use filets of sole
2 shallots, sliced
1/2 bottle dry white wine
1/2 cup cold butter, cut in small pieces
Salt and pepper

Cut spinach, take stems off. Coarsely shred the leaves. Melt butter in fry pan, add shallots and garlic, sauté until soft and fragrant, 1 to 2 minutes. Pack the spinach on top, cover and cook until wilted, stirring often, 2 to 3 minutes. Stir in cream, parsley, lemon zest, nutmeg, salt and pepper and cook without a lid.

Meanwhile work the stale bread into crumbs in a blender. Stir the crumbs into the spinach, taste, and adjust the seasoning. Set stuffing aside to cool.

Preheat oven to 350°.

On the work surface, cut each trout, remove back bone. Place skin side outward, fill center with cooled spinach stuffing. Spread sliced shallots in a medium baking dish. Lay stuffed fish on top of shallots. Don't crowd the fish. Pour in white wine. Cover with foil and bake until fish is no longer transparent when flaked with a fork, 15 to 20 minutes.

Transfer fish to individual serving plates (2 filets per plate) and keep warm.

Strain the cooking liquid into a saucepan and boil it until reduced to about 2 tablespoons of glaze, 8 to 12 minutes. Whisk in the cold butter, a piece at a time, working over low heat until the butter softens and thickens the sauce creamily without melting to oil. Taste and adjust the seasoning. Spoon sauce over fish and serve.

Veal

Veal Scallopini Pecatta or Al Limone

Serves four

1-1/2 lbs. of scallops of veal — 3 per serving
2 tbsp. of olive oil
Salt and pepper
Flour
2 oz. of dry sherry or dry white wine
Juice of 1/2 of a lemon
5 tsp. of capers
1 tbsp. butter
Parsley

Put oil in a sauté pan at medium heat. Salt, pepper, and lightly flour scallops. Then put them, a few at a time, in the sauté pan and cook two to three minutes a side. Remove to warming plate and warm in an oven set at "warm." Sauté the remaining floured and seasoned scallops and add them to the warming plate.

Deglaze the pan with sherry and lemon juice. Add capers and butter, swirl in the pan and pour over the scallops. Sprinkle with parsley. Garnish with lemon wedges dipped in dry parsley.

Accompaniments

Serve with pasta as above for veal scallopini.

Suggestions for vegetables: sliced carrots, green beans, green peas, or sautéed zucchini.

Wine

Serve with Zonata Vallopolicella, a Ricosoli Chianti, or good red Rhône.

Veal Scallopini with Dry Sherry

This is a variation of the familiar Veal Marsala prepared for our friends Duncan and Jean Holt, visiting us from Dallas, Texas. It is quick, simple, and elegant.

Shop for veal scallops at a good butcher (order ahead of time). Have the butcher slice and flatten the veal scallops for sautéing. (If you have to flatten them yourself, place scallops between pieces of wax paper and flatten with a heavy fry pan, other flat object, or rolling pin.)

Serves four

1-1/2 lbs. scallops of veal (3 per person)
Salt and pepper
4 tbsp. flour
2 to 3 tbsp. olive oil
2 oz. dry sherry, divided
8 mushrooms, sliced, 2 per person
1/4 cup fresh parsley, chopped, or 1 tbsp. dried
3 tbsp. butter, divided
1/2 to 1 tbsp. cornstarch or flour

Salt and pepper the scallops, then lightly flour. Heat 2 tbsp. of olive oil in frying pan at medium heat — cook scallops a few at a time 2 to 3 minutes each side, shaking pan, then remove to plate. Place in oven to keep warm. Continue until all of the scallops are cooked adding oil as needed.

Deglaze the pan with 1 to 2 oz. of dry sherry. Scrape up bits on pan bottom. Add 2 tbsp. of butter. Swish in pan — use cornstarch or flour, to thicken if needed.

Sauté sliced mushrooms separately in 1 tsp. of butter, 1/2 tbsp. of olive oil, salt, pepper, 1 oz. of sherry, and parsley.

Combine mushrooms and sauce and pour over veal scallops on plates (three per plate). Sprinkle with parsley.

Accompaniments

Capellini mixed with salt and pepper, 1 tbsp. of olive oil, grated Parmesan or Peccorini or Gruyère — mixed after draining all but 1 cup of cooking water.

Spinach cooked and drained with a splash of olive oil, salt, pepper, grated nutmeg, and squeeze of lemon.

Veal Marengo

Preheat Oven to 350°.

Use the same ingredients as in Chicken Marengo, (page 97) substituting veal stew meat for the chicken. Use meat from the shoulder, neck, short ribs, or what the house affords. Dry the veal and sauté in a tablespoon of olive oil. Place meat in a casserole and toss with flour. Add other ingredients and place in oven for one hour. Baste frequently with pan juices and more white wine if casserole begins to dry.

Accompaniments

Serve with rice or pasta. Sprinkle with chopped parsley. Peas or green beans make a good accompaniment. Some would add black olives, pitted and sliced in half.

Wine

Any good Cabernet Sauvignon, a Ricosoli Chianti Reserva, a Vallopolicella Zonata. Some would like a good rosé. Also suggested: A Côtes du Rhône Guigal. Whites are also in order. A Sokol-Blosser Chardonnay from Dundee, Oregon, would add fullness to the taste buds. Bon appetit!

Emincé de Veau or Zuricher Veal

We first had this dish at Waverly Golf Club as guests of John and Joan O'Connor. On the menu it was listed as "Zuricher Veal," it also is known as "Emincé de Veau."

This dish should be cooked quickly from already prepared and assembled ingredients.

Serves two

1 lb. veal scallops (cut into 2-1/2' x 3/8" x 3/8" strips, pounded to thinness
1/2 cup butter
2 medium to large shallots, peeled and minced
1/8 tsp. dried leaf thyme, crumbled
1/8 tsp. nutmeg, freshly grated (or dried, optional)
1/2 lb. medium mushrooms, wiped clean and thinly sliced
1/2 cup dry white wine
1-1/2 cup heavy cream at room temperature
1/2 tsp. salt, or to taste
1/8 tsp. black ground pepper
Powdered paprika (for color and garnish when plate is set for serving)

Sauté shallots until limp in 1 tbsp of butter and a little oil. Remove to plate to keep warm. Then add another tbsp of butter and some oil to pan. Salt and pepper veal, sauté a few at a time, for about 1/2 minute each side, until scallops all are done. Remove to warming plate.

Deglaze pan with 1/2 cup white wine, stir and scrape meat bits from bottom of pan. Put shallots with any juice back in pan and add mushrooms, thyme and nutmeg. Pour in cream. Restore veal and juice from plate to pan. Heat to moderate. Stir until the sauce thickens.

For garnish shake a little paprika on veal sauce before serving.

Accompaniments

Serve with egg noodles and green beans or peas. Also can be served with Rosti (Swiss hashbrown potatoes).

Vegetables

Asparagus

Simmer in water until tender. Serve hot or cold with lemon butter or any Dijon sauce — simmer until crunchy. Use cold in salads (such as Crab Louis) with mayonnaise, Dijon mustard, lemon juice, capers, or Thousand Island dressing.

Artichokes

1. Boil in water after trimming and removing chokes with a spoon. Serve with lemon mayonnaise or lemon butter.
2. Marinate in oregano, parsley, minced garlic or garlic powder, lemon, white wine vinegar, salt and pepper. Then chill and serve.
3. Small artichoke hearts as in Chicken Bordelaise (see page 95), or marinated with roast chicken — use with marinade.
4. Cold — use in salads.

Cabbage

1. Slice white cabbage and combine with 1/2 cup of water, 1/2 cup of milk, salt, and pepper. Simmer until limp.
2. Slice white cabbage and add to minestrone and vegetable soups.
3. Chop red cabbage and combine with chopped onion; place in a casserole with 1 to 2 tbsp. of butter (you can also use bacon fat). Sprinkle with 3 tbsp. of brown sugar. Pour in 1 cup of red wine and 1 tsp. of

carroway seeds. Add 2 tbsp. of wine vinegar (red or white). Place in oven and cook at 325° for half an hour.

4. Cook with beef roast (not prime rib) in roasting pan in 1/4-inch slices. Baste to keep moist. Roast carrots and onions, etc., in the pan.
5. See recipe for Corned Beef and Cabbage (page 28).

Carrots

1. Glazed: Either slice or use small carrots. Just cover with water and bring to boil. Add 1/2 tsp. of salt and a grind of pepper. Reduce to simmer. Cook 15 to 20 minutes. Test with fork. Drain (leave a little water in pan) and add 1 tbsp. of butter and 1 tbsp. of sugar or brown sugar. Shake pan and cook over low heat until water is evaporated and carrots glaze. Sprinkle with 1/2 tbsp. of dried or fresh, chopped parsley. Cover to keep warm before serving.
2. Creamed: Drain carrots; save water. Mix roux of butter and flour and milk or cream. Use cooking water to make sauce and cream carrots. Also mix with frozen peas.
3. Cut up to cook with roasts, chicken; combine with roast onions and cut-up celery. See Chicken Rio Rico, Pork Roast, Swiss Steak, and stew recipes, etc.

Cauliflower

This white head vegetable is best broken into florets.

1. Steam for 10 to 15 minutes in boiling water, reduced to simmer. Drain, salt and pepper and roll in a patty of butter.

Avoid cooking too long; taste test for a crunchy bite.

2. Heat at low to medium 1/2 cup olive oil. Prepare 1/2 red sweet pepper; clean, slice and dice. Place 1/2 head cauliflower in florets, salt, pepper and red pepper in pan with oil. Cook until crunchy, about 10 minutes.
3. Cook as #1 above and serve with a mornay sauce and a sprinkle of paprika for garnish.

Celery

1. Fresh: Diced or sliced in salads.
2. One-half-inch slices for chicken or beef roasts: Combine with carrots, boil, then add to roast.
3. Braise: Cut celery into 4-inch portions. Tie with string. Braise in beef or chicken stock; drain; salt and pepper. Serve with roasts — chicken or beef or broiled meats. Add cooking broth to gravy, or thicken with flour to make a sauce.

Leeks

This is a simple Vichyssoise. Also serve hot, either unprocessed or blended.

3 to 4 leeks, chopped
1 baking potato, diced
Parsley for garnish
6 cups water
Salt and pepper

Wash leeks well. Chop white parts into small pieces. Put in water with diced potatoes, salt, and pepper. Boil, then simmer. Put into processor to blend; chill. Garnish with fresh parsley.

Add 1 cup of chicken stock for variation — add half and half cream.

Onions

Small Onions

1. Boil two to three minutes, then remove skins and cut stems. Sauté in oil, salt, and pepper; or boil, then simmer. Use in Beef Bourguignon and Blanquette de Veau.
2. Braise small onions in beef or chicken broth, or in oil alone; add herbs and chopped tomatoes, and serve to accompany chicken and fish.
3. Boil until tender. Drain and sauté in 1 tbsp. of butter, 1/2 cup of cream, a little nutmeg,salt, and pepper.

Yellow Onions

1. Peeled, whole, halved or quartered: Use with roasts — beef, chicken, or pork. Brown them with the roasts.
2. Chopped or minced in tomato sauces, etc.
3. Slice yellow onions to put in marinara with chopped garlic and oil to start most tomato-based sauces.
4. Without tomato: Add salt and ground pepper. When onions are translucent, put drained pasta in pan with a cup of cooking water, stirring in the pasta with a spoon. Mix and serve with ground pepper, grated Parmesan and chopped parsley garnish.

Red Onions

Slice thinly for salads.

Scallions

Slice (including some of the greens) for salads or to add to any dish as a substitute where yellow onion is used. Can also be substituted for shallots in most recipes.

Shallots

These are now available in the USA. When I started to cook in 1955, they were hard to find.

1. Use in sauces, etc., instead of onions or scallions and garlic. A milder flavor, favored by the French.
2. Combine shallots and chopped garlic. See use of shallots in chicken poached in butter, in red-wine sauces, and in beef sauces.

Peas

1. Steam with 1/8 head of icebox lettuce, sliced, salt, and pepper.
2. Cook with sliced onion.
3. Cream by themselves or with sliced carrots.

Potatoes

The potato was once the only food for disposessed Irishmen. When the potato had the blight, the Irish endured the infamous famine of 1845–1846. Modern Irish claim a seven course banquet is a sixpack and a baked potato.

Here are some ways to cook the royal spud.

NOTE: Clarified butter: Melt butter and when a milky residue comes to the top, skim it off. Use this butter in sautéing potatoes, etc. The clarified butter will not burn. It is the white, milky residue that turns it to black. Also, when using butter, do not melt it alone; use a little oil in combination with the butter. The quick chef will obtain about the same effect as if only the clarified butter is used.

Au gratin

Use two to three peeled, preboiled, cold potatoes, diced. Grease a Pyrex dish with butter, or part butter and 1 tsp. of oil. Rub plate with diced end of garlic clove or 1 tsp. of minced garlic. When you have filled the dish to the depth of about 1 1/2 inches, salt and pepper and cover with shredded cheddar or other cheese (Swiss, Monterey Jack, Mozzarella). American convention favors cheddar in this dish. Add 1/8th cup milk. Place in preheated oven (at 350°); cook for 15 minutes. Test with fork for doneness, and continue cooking if needed. Putting under the broiler for the last 3 to 5 minutes will add to the golden color.

Boiled

Peel new potatoes and cook in boiling water for about 15 minutes. Drain and then shake in 2 tbsp. of butter, salt, and pepper. Add 2 tbsp. of chopped or 1 tbsp. of dried parsley, if parslied potatoes are desired. Serve hot. If you desire the skins on, scrape both ends, leaving a red center.

Fried

1. Boil two to three baking potatoes until just done (they will be soft when pierced by a fork or knife),

cool and then slice in 1/8-inch slices. Dry slices with a paper towel. Heat about 4 tbsp. of Wesson or other oil in fry pan until very hot but not smoking. Place dried slices in pan and let cook until golden on the panside, then turn with flat spatula to the other side. Test with fork for doneness; they should be soft inside the crust. Remove to paper towel and serve soon or place in oven to warm. (Serving them fresh from the pan ensures flavor.) Sprinkle with salt before serving. Great with eggs, steaks or chops.

2. Panfried and Lyonnaise: Put 1 tbsp. of oil (tbsp. of butter optional) in a frying pan. Heat pan under moderate heat and add one small onion, thinly sliced. Cook until limp, and then add cold, preboiled potatoes, sliced or diced, and fry them in the pan, stirring as they cook. When sautéed to done, you will have potatoes Lyonnaise, named for the famous Burgundian town on the Soane where it joins the Rhône River, one of the great capitals of gastronomy. For variation, add sliced or diced green or red peppers, or both together. Small bits of sliced ham will also be a good addition, sautéed with the other ingredients. (Here we are not limited by orthodoxy in cuisine, but left to new initiatives and combinations.)

Mashed

Slice peeled baking potatoes in 1/4-inch slices and boil until tender. Drain potatoes and let steam to dry a bit. Then mash, adding 1/4 cup of warm milk and 2 tbsp. of butter. Mash further until fluffy. If garlic mashed potatoes are desired, cook peeled cloves of one head of garlic in 1/4 cup of milk, then mix with the mashed potatoes. Salt and pepper. Watch the milk; avoid getting potatoes too watery.

Roast

Slice baking potatoes into 1/4-inch slices, salt and pepper, roll in olive oil, and place in Pyrex dish in 350° oven for 30 to 40 minutes, shaking or stirring the dish frequently to avoid sticking to pan. Red potatoes cut in half, rolled in olive oil, salt and peppered, can also be roasted. Sprinkling with dry rosemary is another variation. Place potatoes in roasting pan with chicken or meat roasts and cook with the meat, with or without other vegetables such as carrots, celery, turnips, etc.

Scalloped

Use the recipe for scalloped potatoes found in the Black Forest Ham recipe in this book on page 69. For four people, use two to three baking potatoes, peeled and sliced in 1/8-inch slices. Use Swiss, Parmesan, Mozzarella, Gruyère, Monterey Jack, or a mixture of these. The cheese can be either grated or sliced, since it will melt while cooking. Also, as the potatoes cook they will acquire a golden color. Watch for this about 30 minutes into the cooking, and test for doneness with the tines of a fork. Dot each tier of potatoes liberally with butter. Cook a little extra, since they will make a good luncheon accompaniment cold or reheated. Alternatives: a cup of chicken or beef broth may be substituted for the milk and cooked down in the same way.

Sauces

Odori

As a Tuscan basic sauce mixture, it is called "odori." It is a basis for pasta, soups, stews, and sauces. Its ingredients are extended into sauces such as "Bolognese."

1 tbsp. of olive oil
2 carrots, finely chopped
1 stalk of celery, finely chopped
1 cup of chopped parsley (1 tbsp. dried)
1 cup of red onion, sliced fine (yellow onion will do; optional)

Sauté the vegetables over medium heat until they are limp and oil is absorbed. Then proceed to use to make sauce or soup, or use as base for sautés and stews.

Sauce Bolognese

In the early 1980s, I was in Jiddah, Saudi Arabia. My friend Dave Scott and I were billeted at the Sheraton Hotel in this Arab city on the Red Sea. The Islamic prohibition against the consumption of pork caused my bacon and eggs to be made with phony bacon. Also, the cuisine seemed limited, but a staple of the menu was "Spaghetti Bolognese." Dave and I ordered it every night and followed it with vanilla ice cream. Despite the Jiddah memory, I still like Bolognese.

Here is a recipe for this famous sauce. Serve with spaghetti or other pasta. The missing pork is added here — but if you wish, substitute ground chicken breast.

Serves eight to ten

1/4 cup of olive oil
1 medium onion, finely diced
1 medium carrot, finely diced
1 medium celery salk, finely diced
1 oz. of sliced bacon (2 to 3 slices), finely diced (Italians use "pancetta")
2 large garlic cloves, chopped fine
1/4 pound ground veal
1/4 pound ground pork
1/4 pound ground beef
3/4 cup of white wine
1 28-oz. can of peeled or diced tomatoes
1 cup of chicken stock
1 bay leaf
Salt and freshly ground pepper
1/2 cup of cream
1/8 tsp. of dried thyme
Spaghetti or pasta
Ground or grated Parmesan for serving with spaghetti

Sauté bits of bacon in pan, then add the vegetables, garlic, and onions in oil, and sauté at medium heat, stirring from time to time until softened. Remove mixture to a bowl; add more olive oil. Sauté ground meats, mixing them about five minutes; do not brown. Then return vegetables to the pan and stir together. Add the wine. Cook five to six minutes, then add the tomatoes, chicken stock, thyme, and bay leaf and bring to boil. Reduce heat to simmer; cook one to one and one-half hours. Add cream and heat through. Serve over pasta with grated Parmesan cheese on the side.

Dry Beans

Kidney, navy, garbanzo, cici (northern white beans), cannellini (larger than northern) are great food. A bag of dried beans takes very little storage space, and when cooked, can be used in salads, mixed with pasta, added to tomato and other sauces, in soups and in many other ways. With a vinegarette, garbanzos are a tasteful antipasto.

Soak the dried beans over night or for a few hours at least. The canned varieties serve as well.

String Beans

1. Cook until al dente (crunchy), drain, and add salt and ground pepper. Heat fry pan with 1 tbsp. olive oil, add finely chopped garlic, raise heat, then lower it. Stir garlic for one or two minutes (don't burn), then add beans. Shake pan and coat beans. Turn off heat and cover pan until time to serve. Or, alternatively, drain and refresh beans, add 1/2 tbsp. olive oil to pot and 1/4 tsp. garlic powder, raise heat and shake pan for 1 to 2 minutes. Remove from heat, salt and pepper, cover pan to keep beans warm.
2. With roast chicken or meats, add string beans halfway through roasting and mix with other vegetables.
3. Cream as with carrots, or mix with carrots.

Tomatoes

1. Diced in marinara (tomato sauces)
2. Cut and broiled with oregano, basil, parsley, Parmesan, olive oil, bread crumbs. Add to fish, roasts, chicken, lamb, or beef.
3. Fresh: Dress with vinaigrette, fresh basil and Mozzarella in tomato-onion salad.
4. As a garnish when broiled or roasted.
5. Dice and mix in stews (Navarin, etc.).

Tomato-Onion Salad

3 tomatoes
1 onion
1/2 cup fresh parsley or 1 tbsp. dried
1 clove garlic, minced
4 to 5 leaves Romaine lettuce
1/2 cup vinaigrette dressing
1 tbsp. oregano, dried
1/2 cup fresh basil cut into small pieces, or 1 tbsp. dried basil

Slice tomatoes, thinly slice and chop onions, or use slices only (optional). Place tomatoes on a bed of lettuce leaves; salt and pepper. Strew onions, minced garlic, and basil on tomatoes. Sprinkle oregano also, or mix extra oregano in vinaigrette. Place in refrigerator and serve as soon as possible. Dress with vinaigrette.

Use the vinaigrette dressing on page 11.

More Food History — Pizza and Caprese

In 1939 I was living on the campus at Fordham College in the Bronx. Just south of there, across Fordham Road, was the Italian neighborhood, mostly Sicilian, called "Arthur Avenue." Twice a week the street was given over to push-cart vegetable stands. The used crates were burned in the street at night, just like in Mario Puzzo's "Godfather." The neighborhood church had popcorn like lightbulbs outlining the building at night when lit to celebrate, adding a festive note on feast days. In his book Puzzo has several meetings of the mob dons take place in Arthur Avenue.

Here I was introduced to "La Beetz" by Ray Mazzocane, my Scicilian classmate from New Haven. "La Beetz" in the 1960s became famous as pizza. Frankie Ierulli of Portland, introduced pizza to Portland through "Shakey's Pizza Parlours" in the 1960s. Pizza is now as American as the hot dog. So, "La Beetz" has come a long way in America since 1939, when it came from a baker's brick and stucco oven in "Arthur Avenue."

In 1996 I took Ginney to Arthur Avenue and had Caprese at Amelia's Restaurant. It was a good beginning of a leisurely Italian lunch and a nostalgic return to my youth at Fordham.

Caprese — Insalata Di Pomadori É Mozzarella

Tomato and Mozzarella Salad with Fresh Basil

Arrange sliced tomatoes and a slice of fresh mozzarella, on top, over a broad leaf of Romaine or other leaf lettuce. Season with a shake of salt and two grinds of black pepper, and put chopped fresh basil on top. The drizzle with Ryan Vinaigrette, see page 11.

Turnips

1. Peel and cut off at base. Quarter and cook with roast meats or chicken.
2. Use in stews. See Lamb Navarin (page 19) and Beef Stew American Style (page 17). Boil and then puree; combine with 1 tbsp. of butter, salt, and pepper. Also, combine with mashed potatoes. This goes well with roasts, lamb or broiled chicken.
3. Pureed (turnips only): Mix with butter, salt and pepper.

Zucchini

This delicious squash has many cooking possibilities. It cooks quickly; if overcooked, it becomes soft and loses its crunchiness. Some suggestions:

Slice zucchini. Cook one half of an onion, finely sliced, and one clove of finely chopped garlic, in 2 tbsp. of olive oil over low heat until they are soft. (Do not brown or burn.) Add zucchini, with 1 tsp. of salt and several grinds of pepper. Sprinkle with 1/2 tbsp. dried oregano (or substitute 1/2 tbsp. dried dill), some chopped fresh parsley, or 1/2 tbsp. dried parsley. Cook at low heat, stirring or shaking in pan. Do not overcook.

Variations

1. Add one 14.5-oz. can of diced tomatoes, or one whole tomato cut into 1/8-inch pieces. Use fresh

basil with other herbs, if available, with tomatoes.

2. One to 2 oz. of dry sherry will also add to the flavor and moisten the mix. Pour the sherry into the pan halfway through cooking. Cooking time in all should be 15 to 20 minutes.
3. Dill is also a good herb to flavor zucchini.
4. With crooked neck yellow squash, slice one squash and one zucchini. Sauté as above.
5. Zucchini also is delicious sautéed with sliced mushrooms.
6. For variety, add sliced Mozzarella or powdered Parmesan and melt over zucchini.
7. Add to vegetables with roasts, but add toward the end of cooking to avoid overcooking.

Last Word

Please accept these recipes as an invitation to culinary adventures. The measurements, the "how to do" are not fixed rules, but happy guidelines to good cooking.

Last of all, mothers and fathers, if you have not done so, revive the great institution of the family meal. It is a way to teach manners, how to use a knife and fork, and the art of conversation. Here's to a happy kitchen and happy families.

John D. Ryan.